HELPING THE FAMILY IN URBAN SOCIETY

HELPING THE FAMILY
IN URBAN SOCIETY

EDITED BY FRED DELLIQUADRI

NEW YORK AND LONDON

COLUMBIA UNIVERSITY PRESS

HQ
537
.N3
1962

Copyright © 1963
National Conference on Social Welfare
Columbus, Ohio

First printing 1963
Third printing 1968

Library of Congress Catalog Card Number: 63-9804
Printed in the United States of America

FOREWORD

EACH YEAR the National Conference selects a theme that reflects the significant goals of social welfare as they relate to the environment of the time. The 1962 theme, "Social Goals of a Free Society," was developed by the principal speakers and reflected by all the participants in the Conference.

In addition, it has become the practice of the Program Committee to select one or more aspects of the general theme for intensive treatment. It was evident in the early discussions of the committee that the special topic for consideration should reflect a concern for families and children. An appropriate title, "Strengthening the Family for Children," was chosen to express the most important social goal of our society. With this directive the Division program for the Conference took shape quickly. In considering the serious implications of such a vast topic, the Division Committee charged with the development of meetings on the subject agreed that the meetings should focus on the identification and analysis of social factors that affect today's family life adversely or contribute to its strengthening. Additional emphasis would be on the development of proposals for study or action to prevent breakdown or to increase strength, including the cooperation of social work with the other disciplines concerned with social welfare.

To set the stage for a number of meetings, it was agreed

that a broad philosophical discussion was needed dealing with the family, not only from an historical aspect, but to discuss current concepts of the family and goals for the family. Dr. Charles Frankel, of Columbia University, consented to undertake this difficult task, and his address, "The Family in Context," reveals a keen and penetrating insight. His thesis: "The family in Western society was once the principal agency for the performance of what are now called welfare functions; it is now the principal target of these functions. It has been converted from the doctor to the patient. What is involved in this change? What has caused it? What new attitudes and what new social conceptions are required to deal effectively with this problem?" In exploring these questions, Dr. Frankel provides a philosophical base for a social work program in a most exciting way. His description of the role of the family provides the basis of our conviction that service to families and social work services must be identical. A careful analysis of his speech is warranted by all social workers.

Dr. Frankel's session provided the foundation for eight large concurrent sessions that followed in the morning, as well as five additional sessions in the afternoon of the same day. Limitation of space allow only fourteen of the important papers of these sessions to be published in this volume. They reflect in a most dramatic way the paradoxes and the challenges of contemporary society, the confusion and pressures in today's families, and the cores of strength in family life for the individual and society. These were presented, analyzed, and assessed in relation to home, neighborhood design, employment patterns, recreational patterns, educational patterns, unequal opportunities, and mass media.

The enthusiastic response of the various audiences indicated that the theme, the pattern of its development, the manner of presentation, and the use of various disciplines was highly commendable and most productive. The Chairman was extremely indebted to a hard-working committee as well as to the financial support of the Marion Ascoli Fund, the National Institute of Mental Health, and the Taconic Foundation for the development and presentation of the program.

Mrs. Dorothy Bird Daly, of the New York University Graduate School of Social Work, deserves special mention for her staff services to the Committee. In conclusion, the Committee recommends careful reading of this volume because it feels that the contents represent a great contribution to social work literature in knowledge, understanding, and action.

FRED DELLIQUADRI
Chairman of the Division Program

New York, New York
November, 1962

CONTENTS

THE CONTRIBUTORS

ALINE B. AUERBACH, Assistant Director, Child Study Association of America, New York

GRACE HOLMES BARBEY, UNICEF Liaison Office, United Nations, New York

BERTRAM M. BECK, Associate Executive Director, National Association of Social Workers, New York

CLARK W. BLACKBURN, General Director, Family Service Association of America, New York

DOROTHY BIRD DALY, Director of Field Work, Graduate School of Social Work, New York University, New York

JOSEPH P. FITZPATRICK, S.J., Chairman, Department of Sociology and Anthropology, Fordham University, New York

CHARLES FRANKEL, Professor of Philosophy, Columbia University, New York

ELINOR GUGGENHEIMER, President, National Committee for the Day Care of Children, New York

ROBERT J. HAVIGHURST, Professor of Education, University of Chicago, Chicago

MARIANA JESSEN, Executive Director, National Committee for the Day Care of Children, New York

PIERRE JOHANNET, M.D., James Jackson Putnam Children's Center, Boston

CYRUS H. KARRAKER, Professor of History, Bucknell University, Lewisburg, Pa.

NORMAN V. LOURIE, Deputy Secretary, Pennsylvania State Department of Public Welfare, Harrisburg

JESSIE E. PEEKE, Project Director, Council of Community Services, San Bernardino, California

JOSEPH H. REID, Executive Director, Child Welfare League of America, New York

SISTER SERENA, Administrator, Kennedy Child Study Center, New York

LAURA LEE SPENCER, Women's Bureau, Legislation Division, United States Department of Labor, Washington, D.C.

RUTH S. TEFFERTELLER, Program Director, Henry Street Settlement, New York

CHARLOTTE TEJESSY, presently associated with the Jewish Board of Guardians, New York; formerly Associate in Psychiatric Social Work, Division of Psychiatry, Boston University—Massachusetts Memorial Hospitals, Boston

HELEN M. WALLACE, M.D., Professor of Maternal and Child Health, School of Public Health, University of California, Berkeley; formerly Chief, Child Health Studies Branch, Division of Research, Children's Bureau, Department of Health, Education, and Welfare, Washington, D.C.

ELIZABETH WOOD, Director of Urban Studies, Management Services Associates, Inc., New York

HELPING THE FAMILY
IN URBAN SOCIETY

THE FAMILY IN CONTEXT

by Charles Frankel

ONE OF THE PARADOXES of contemporary sociology is that the family has been studied as much, perhaps, as any institution in our society, and yet the theoretical organization and development of the voluminous materials that have been gathered are even more conspicuously absent than in other fields of sociological inquiry.[1] Indeed, there is no great classic in twentieth-century sociology, comparable to Max Weber's study of bureaucracy or even to Veblen's studies of business enterprise and the leisure class, that is devoted to the institution which is, by common consent, the principal matrix for the formation of individual personality and the most cherished institution of our civilization.

As a philosopher, I can claim no special knowledge of the family, and what I propose to put before you is certainly much less than a theory of the family. I wish to discuss two questions. First, what are the fundamental changes in our institutions and attitudes that have affected the family and produced the situation in which we now find it? Second, what is the value of the family, the purpose, that is to say, which we should have in mind when we say that the family

[1] See William J. Goode, "The Sociology of the Family," in Robert K. Merton, Leonard Broom and Leonard S. Cottrell, Jr., eds., *Sociology Today* (New York: Basic Books, 1959), pp. 178–96.

is worth preserving and strengthening, and when we set about trying to do so?

Let me begin by stating the thesis which I wish to demonstrate and explore: the family in Western society was once the chief agency for the performance of what are now called welfare functions; it is now the chief target of these functions. It has been converted from the doctor to the patient. What is involved in this change? What has caused it? What new attitudes and what new social conceptions are required to deal effectively with this problem?

The answers to these questions lie in a complex of radical changes which have taken place in Western society over the last three or four hundred years. Among these are the shift from an agricultural subsistence economy to a commercial economy; industrialization; the steady movement of displaced rural people to the cities; the "Americanization" of culture; the rise of liberal ideas concerning the proper relation of the individual to the social groups in which he is born or to which he becomes attached; and last, the democratization of the once aristocratic ideal of romantic love. A glance at each of these may help us to see the problem of the family in its context.

The shift from an agricultural subsistence economy to a commercial economy is a first step in the major secular trend that has marked the development of the modern family. That trend consists in the steady expulsion of the family from the economy and, in a certain sense, from society. In traditional agricultural societies, the family is an economic unit, a social instrument of production. Children, especially male children, are economically profitable rather than burdensome. And large, extended families, consisting of grandparents, uncles, aunts, cousins and in-laws, as well as children, are forms of social insurance, the basic protection against the blows of sickness, old age, and outrageous fortune. Accordingly, the individual's experience within his family is at the same time his principal experience of society at large. In giving him his name, the family also gives him his place—usually his lifetime place—in society. It is as a member of a family that the individual not merely learns his social roles but acquires them. And it is within his family that he does the work of the world.

The commercialization of the economy, in contrast, brings strangers together. It begins to separate the home from the economy and, indeed, to give the home its modern meaning as a refuge from practical problems rather than a device for dealing with these problems. Commercialization, furthermore, brings in its train standard instruments of exchange, like money; impersonal instruments of social control, like the police and government officials; uniform and explicit rules and regulations, like delivery schedules, piecework rates, and systems of cost accounting. These may not quite destroy the traditional powers of the elders of the clan or the habit of treating one's kinsmen differently from the stranger. But they break into such powers and habits and put them under pressure to justify themselves. The traditional family is held together by a system of authority based largely on one's "natural"—which is to say, culturally inherited—status as the elder or the father. The commercialization of a society begins to introduce the notion that status and authority are acquired by performance rather than simply ascribed. Traditional notions of authority based on the family lose their monopolistic position. Internal authority within the family is affected.

The industrialization of society immensely quickened

this process. As a student of the industrialization of modern China has remarked, "modern industry and the 'traditional' family are mutually subversive." [2] Industrialization
took work and father away from the home. Just as much
to the point, it took women and children out of the home,
and affected the position of the male as the director of the
economic and educational life of the family. Industrialization tends to change the traditional extended family from a
necessity to a source of irritation. Viewed from the standpoint of industrialization, the traditional extended family
makes mobility more difficult; it enlarges the circle of de-
pendents for whom the individual is responsible; it limits
his associations and circumscribes the activities in which he
ought to participate if he wishes to improve his condition.
Not least, the traditional extended family preserves the idea
that the old have a function to serve in the family; industrialism, in contrast, declares the old obsolete.

Industrialization, furthermore, is in part the invention of
techniques for invention, and perhaps the deepest of its
effects lies in the steadily accelerating tempo of social change
which it creates. It produces a world in which the generations feel more separate, more distant, from one another,
and creates reasonable doubts in both parents and children
that the old can teach the young useful lessons in how to
make their way in the world. Even a hundred years ago,
the grandmother who knew her place was a matriarch. Now,
if she is lucky and moves as though she were treading on
eggshells, she may just qualify as a friend. No doubt there
have always been quarrels between children and parents.

[2] Marion J. Levy, Jr., *The Family Revolution in Modern China*
(Cambridge, Mass.: Harvard University Press, 1949), p. 354.

But industrialization, for better or worse, makes this a structural feature of human history.

Nor is this all. Industrialization is linked with urbanization, which reinforces the tendencies toward the miniaturization of the family and the loosening of the bonds within it. The living space in cities is crowded and expensive, and particularly so for those families undergoing the stresses of cultural transition. Quite simply, the large family, stretching over more than two generations, does not ordinarily fit into city apartments; or, if it is made to fit, the fit is painful and can be the source of new and steady frictions. Moreover, the dwellers in cities are mobile, physically and psychologically. They go where the jobs are, and their minds move in wider orbits. Their ties to a particular neighborhood or to their own parental family are weaker as a consequence. Cities are towns with floating populations; and they are also the scenes of a recurrent drama—the conflict between the first generation of new arrivals and the second generation, which has rejected the old traditions and is tempted or frightened by, resentful of or greedy for, the life that lies beyond the ghetto.

Nor are commerce, technology, and industry the only factors that produce social mobility and the mobile personality. Social mobility, movement up and down the social ladder, is of course immensely accelerated by industrialism. But something else, something nonmaterial, has also changed men's perspectives and expectations, particularly in the United States. One of the classic functions of the traditional family is simply to give the individual a name, and with that name his status for life. But the recurrent theme of the modern novel, from the time of Cervantes, is the story of the man who gives himself a name, who aspires to a position to which he has no inherited right. The familial outlook, the outlook that puts each person in his proper place by looking at his origins, is in conflict with the industrial and democratic outlook, which treats a man's status as something to be acquired and earned.

Nowhere has this attitude gone farther than in the United States. Defined in strict and narrow terms—in terms, for example, of the movement of children of manual workers to white-collar jobs—social mobility is not significantly higher in the United States than in other highly industrialized countries. But in America social mobility is expected and perceived; Americans believe that the process takes place, and they believe in the process. They believe, that is to say, that it is the major mechanism for achieving social justice; the achievement of social justice by conflict between social classes made up of people locked into position inside their class has not usually occurred to them and has practically never appealed to them. This is part of a characteristic and persisting American style, one that can be detected very early in our history and one which has not greatly altered despite all that has happened to the structure of American society.

This, if you will, is the Americanization of culture, the acid that has corroded traditional social relationships since the colonization of North America and the emergence of the American Republic. Perhaps more than anything else, it is what America represented to the imaginations of restless millions in the nineteenth century. "The young American," said Max Weber, "has no respect for anything or anybody, for tradition or for public office—unless it is for the personal achievement of individual men. This is what the American calls 'democracy.' " [3] And Baedeker's guide warily warned the European traveler coming to this country at the turn of the century that he "should, from the outset, reconcile himself to the absence of deference, of servility, on the part of those he considers his social inferiors." [4]

The effects of this attitude on the traditional patterns of authority within the family were noted long before John Dewey came on the scene, or popular versions of the doctrines of a Viennese doctor made "permissiveness" the rationale for a new form of tyranny in the home. "The theory of the equality of man is rampant in the nursery," a British visitor to the United States remarked in 1898.[5] And Arthur Calhoun has documented the changes that took place in the American family long before the Civil War.[6] The Americanization of culture meant a change in normal attitudes within the family: it meant a shift from a past-oriented family to a future-oriented one; from a parent-oriented family to a child-oriented and, some think, to a childishly oriented, family. In older societies a man took pride in his son if he could imagine his son coming to share some of his own adult burdens, carrying his load in the family, carrying on the family in its name and its traditional work. In modern societies, and overwhelmingly in modern American society, fathers look to their sons to lift the family, to renovate it,

[3] "Science as a Vocation," in H. H. Gerth and C. Wright Mills, eds., *From Max Weber* (New York: Oxford University Press, 1946), p. 149.

[4] Quoted by Seymour M. Lipset, "A Changing American Character?" Institute of Industrial Relations, Reprint No. 180, University of California, 1962.

[5] James F. Muirhead, *The Land of Contrasts* (Boston and New York: 1898), quoted by Lipset, *op. cit.*

[6] Arthur W. Calhoun, *A Social History of the American Family from Colonial Times to the Present* (Cleveland: Arthur H. Clark Co., 1918).

to make it something it has not been before. And that
orientation is arising rapidly in other societies today. The
much discussed "revolution of rising expectations" is in the
first instance a demand on the part of countless men and
women that their children have a chance for an education
which they did not have. It represents a revolution in what
men and women want for their children, in the way in which
they perceive their relations to their children and the rightful prospects of their children—a revolution, in a word, in
the way in which they think about the nature and function
of the family itself.

Closely connected with this Americanization of culture
is the influence of the liberal revolution in ideas that began
in the seventeenth century, that came to full intellectual
expression in the eighteenth, and that changed the social
map of Europe and America in the nineteenth. In its moral
aspect, this revolution spoke for a simple idea: the idea that
all authority exercised by human beings over other human
beings is only provisional authority—fallible, limited, subject to reversal when it fails to serve the functions for which
it exists. It was and is a radical idea, one that had been
glimpsed and expounded previously but never happily
adopted as a guide for the organization of large societies
and the government of men in all classes. In its social aspects, it implied a profound change in the relation of the
individual to the groups to which he belongs.

It meant that the ideal relationship was normally con-
strued as one that was revocable and alterable, a relationship that the individual could choose, and could continue
to choose, for himself. The elimination of fixed feudal bonds,
the protection of freedom of association and of the right to
pick up and move, the easing of divorce laws, the attack on

restrictive practices in inheritance, the protection of the rights of children, are all examples of this process. The liberal revolution could not quite make the family an entirely voluntary association. No one can choose his parents, or his sisters, cousins, and aunts, no matter what the law may do to enhance his freedom of choice as a citizen. But the liberal revolution went a long way in changing the family from a wholly hereditary grouping into one with many more elements of voluntary association in it. It reinforced, and was reinforced by, the material changes that were also transforming the family and converting it from a major instrument for the protection of individuals and the assignment of social status and function to only one instrument among many.

Finally, a change in moral attitudes must be noted. The word "love" is a dangerous word to define, and as those who remember their Plato will recall, philosophers particularly have done remarkable things with the word and to it. But for our prosaic purposes we may define it, perhaps, as an intense attraction between two people (presumably erotic in its character) which leads them, for a period of unspecified duration, to wish to organize their lives and their emotions around it. Now some recent social theorists, bravely setting themselves against the notion that everything is learned at the bosom of "culture," that men and women have no ideas of their own where their instincts are concerned, have gone so far as to argue that this inconvenient feeling breaks out in all societies and causes trouble in most.[7] This may be; at any rate, I am not querulous enough to argue against this mournful though somehow encouraging speculation. Nevertheless, no student of human societies has as

[7] See Goode, *op. cit.*

yet denied that we in Western civilization have developed
a special cult around the idea of love, and that in this cult
—the cult of romantic love—instinct has combined with
imagination to make trouble for parents, priests, bankers,
socialists, and everyone else who favors a sensible, business-
like approach to human affairs.

The cult of romantic love, to cut a long story very short,
holds that nothing is more important than love, that love
justifies all.[8] It is the secularized and materialized version of
Dante's religious attitude toward Beatrice, whom he trans-
figured into a representative of the supernatural, a guide who
could show him the way through Paradise. This is a heavy
burden for one human being to place on another; and in
the early historical career of romantic love, it was conceived
as a relationship best maintained by keeping the lovers at a
distance, a relationship that was more a matter of mind
than of matter. What we now know as romantic love began,
indeed, as courtly love, which in its standard form was the
unconsummated love of a bachelor knight for an aristocratic
married lady. In its second stage, it was adulterous love,
based on the notion that love and marriage, to diverge from
contemporary wisdom, go together like a wild horse and carriage. But this was too much, as one can imagine, for the
bourgeois soul. When the middle classes took over the world,
they took over romantic love and domesticated it. It was
conceived as an emotion properly felt only between two
otherwise uncommitted individuals, and the proper pre-
lude to marriage. In short, romantic love, which began as
an aristocratic affair providing an outlet from marriage, has

[8] For a general account of the cult and culture of love, see Morton
M. Hunt, *The Natural History of Love* (New York: Alfred A. Knopf,
1959).

ended as a plebeian affair which, in theory, is the only good reason for marriage. The cult of romantic love caps and sanctifies the great transformation in the meaning of marriage in Western society. From a practical and useful alliance of two families it has been converted into an alliance between two individuals with respect to which, so a major ethical ideal of our culture tells us, it is somehow improper and unfeeling to ask questions about practicality and use.

These, then, are some of the long-range developments that have altered the meaning and function of the family in our civilization. During the last generation a variety of other changes have still further complicated the problem. I can list only some of them. Domestic servants have largely disappeared from middle-class homes. A larger number of women are working. The lowering of the retirement age and the technological displacement of older workers have cut still further into the authority within the family once enjoyed by the elders of the tribe. Wars have increased mobility, quick marriages, long separations, and the general atmosphere of unease and insecurity. The mass media of communication have moved into the home itself, changing the character of the time that families spend together. And as a result of labor laws that keep youth out of the employment market, and of technical innovations which require that workers have longer and longer periods of schooling, the episode in life we know as youth, the time between arrival at biological maturity and arrival at a recognized status as an independent adult, has been greatly extended—so much so that problems we could once sweep under the carpet, problems affecting our touchiest moral beliefs, can no longer be ignored. A larger number of those who can afford to do so marry young, taking a more frankly experimental view of marriage. Those who cannot afford the proprieties, or who take marriage too seriously to marry lightly, make other arrangements, and except for occasional ceremonial outbursts most of us look the other way.[9]

But perhaps the greatest assault on our peace of mind comes from the simple fact that the dominant ideal of the family—the middle-class ideal of the secure family of firmly married parents with two or three children, living in a community of more or less permanent residence—this ideal, though we cling to it, is more conspicuously unrelated to the facts than ever before. Not only does it mislead us about the facts, but it imposes a single standard, and often an unrealistic and confusing standard, on the great variety of conditions and relationships that characterize families today. On the one side we have no developed intellectual theories about the family; on the other side, we are in the grip of massive stereotypes. We speak of *"the* family" as though we knew just what we meant and as though there were only one kind of entity to which it referred.

In fact, "the family" is a term that covers a wide range of disparate phenomena. There is the traditional extended family and the small, nuclear family. There is the nuclear family in which the parents are divorced; the family in which the parents are officially separated; the family in which they are neither separated nor *not* separated, but only intermittently together; the family in which one parent is dead; the foster family; the family in which the children have never known their father; the family in which, as a result of divorce and remarriage, there are two fathers or two mothers. And within all these different varieties—and there

[9] For a study of changing sexual mores, see Ira L. Reiss, *Premarital Sexual Standards in America* (Glencoe, Ill.: Free Press, 1960).

are others as well—there are further differences in ethnic origin and social class which affect the roles of parents and children and the tone and content of family life. Indeed, one of the greatest problems affecting the future welfare of what we choose to call "the family" is the persistence of the notion that there is one proper model for the family, and that all efforts to repair the condition of the family should be guided by this single conception of what it is to be a proper family.

In sum, the trials and tribulations of modern families arise, for the most part, because modern social arrangements have stripped the family of many of its traditional functions and patterns of authority, while, at the same time, modern moral attitudes have greatly raised the emotional demands we make upon the family. The situation invites a basic question: What is the value of the family? In trying to preserve family institutions, are we simply trying to preserve old superstitions? It is worth asking this radically skeptical question. It may help us to be clearer about the reasons behind any programs we may wish to institute to strengthen the family.

Most of the answers that are given to this question, it seems to me, are not quite to the point. It is true that families do many important things. They provide emotional support for their members, the opportunity for sexual gratification, a setting for the birth, nurturing, and rearing of children; in all probability, they are the most important agencies in our society for the molding of personality and the social control of individual behavior, particularly among the young. But families are not alone in serving these functions; and many families do not fulfill such functions, or fulfill them badly. Assuming that we had no deep-seated religious and moral attitudes toward the family, can we be sure that some other sort of institution might not do better?

To ask this question is to bring out, I think, the root element in the concept of "family." It is the simple idea of kinship. Families are groups of people connected by ties of blood. Even the existence of the institution of adoption, which simulates kinship, emphasizes this point. What the family does distinctively is to give the individual a name, a plain and ineffaceable tie to generations past and future, a unique locale in society. A man's family is like the color of his eyes or, if you prefer, like the birthmark on his face. He can like it or hate it, exploit it or disguise it or perform a kind of surgery to get rid of it; but it is one of the arbitrary facts of his life. He has to live with it or take positive and painful steps to live without it. The family, the kin group, gives support to some people; it is a nuisance to others and a disaster to some. But whatever its effects on the individual, it is not a relationship which can just be assumed or rejected. A man can leave his job and that is his own business; he can make friendships and break them, and that too is his business. But while he can leave his family or ignore his parents or children, that is not just his business. In the family he finds a kind of relationship to others that is not so easily altered as his other relationships, a set of obligations that are not provisional but categorical. The kin group gives the individual other people to whom he belongs and who belong to him, whether he likes it or not.

In short, the family introduces into our increasingly rationalized society an element of sheer inescapable contingency and individuality. More and more of our social arrangements assign interchangeable individuals to general social tasks; the worth of our arrangements is measured in terms of precisely defined utilities; the positions we occupy or the jobs we perform rest on our specific skills and services, real or alleged; the groups to which we belong are supposed to contribute to our advantage and we to theirs. The family, in contrast, envelops the individual in a network of relationships that are not just matters of *quid pro quo,* that do not fit any engineer's plan or respond to any simple conception of efficiency. It is impossible to tell what this means for the individual's sense of himself or for his outlook on the world, but we may be certain that some of our most fundamental moral ideas and some of our most deep-seated habits of feeling would be changed if we created institutions that served the other functions that families serve, but which eliminated the idea of kinship.

Tocqueville talked of the awful loneliness of individualism and democracy, which throws the individual "back forever upon himself alone and threatens in the end to confine him entirely within the solitude of his own heart." [10] It is the family which protects most of us against this solitude and engages us, drafts us, into the sorrows and joys of our world. So long as it exists for a child or an adult, their world is not entirely impersonal, not entirely bureaucratized, at least a little individualized and personally accented. The justice appropriate to the relations between kinsmen, as Aristotle observed, is not the same as the justice appropriate to relations simply between fellow citizens. Since the time of Descartes philosophers have made the effort to build moral systems *de novo,* as though they were building geometries based on universal and abstract axioms. Perhaps the simplest reason why such efforts were bound to fail is that families

[10] Alexis de Tocqueville, *Democracy in America,* Phillips Bradley, ed. (New York: Alfred A. Knopf, 1945), II, 99.

exist. So long as they do exist, men cannot build up their obligations by a free act of mind or will. They do not have to decide to be "engaged" or "committed." They are born into a network of *prima facie* obligations, and of affections and disaffections, which are specific and concrete. They begin their moral lives *in medias res*.

This may all be rather obvious, but it helps explain and, I think, justifies a conception that has been present in the development of contemporary welfare programs—the conception that, if it is at all possible, families should be held together and help to children should be given within the family context. For the idea of family, of kinship, is one of the root ideas that holds together and penetrates a great many of our moral conceptions. And this brings us back to the radical changes in Western institutions which have made us anxious and perplexed about the future of the family.

History, pursued too far, can be an escape from a problem, not an introduction to it. I have not dwelt on the great historical trends which have affected the character and position of the modern American family in order to add my voice to the many others which proclaim that our civilization has simply taken the wrong road, and that the problems faced by contemporary families can only be solved by reversing the major directions of change that have marked the development of contemporary society. Such views are exactly analogous to complaints that the invention of the motorcar is the cause of the increase in serious traffic accidents. They confuse the context in which a problem arises with its cause, and they do not solve the problem but wash it away in a flood of empty and indignant words. The long-range changes in social organization that have altered the nature and function of the family cannot be reversed. And just as much to the point, if they could be reversed, few of us would wish to do so. They are changes which, in their net effects, have greatly increased the freedom of choice available to individuals and have provided the setting for a new kind of human experience, an experience more various, more self-conscious, more intense. They are changes, in short, which we normally applaud and to which we are morally committed. The question is whether we can find ways to make our commitment to these changes compatible with our commitment to the ideas and institutions of kinship.

There can be little doubt that this process of adaptation has hardly begun. Social attitudes that are still dominant among us with regard to the family are, in the main, anachronisms. It is argued, to take some conspicuous examples, that the problem of care for the aged is a private problem for individual families; that illegitimate children are a private problem; that delinquency is caused simply by the failure of parents to exercise proper authority in the home; that the decline of self-reliance, respect for motherhood, and all the other fine old values—and some of them are fine even if old—are due to the fact that we have strangely lost faith and are teaching our children the wrong things. Such arguments assume that parents are not as bewildered as their children by change; that if father is a ne'er-do-well or mother is ill, there is always an uncle or an aunt standing by; that authority can be exercised inside the home without regard to pressures outside the home; that self-reliance can be taught when there are no legitimate opportunities for its exercise. They make the comforting, but untrue, assumption, in short, that we still inhabit a static society of small communities and large, self-sufficient families.

Undoubtedly, the weaknesses of individuals, their igno-

rance, their impulsiveness, their indiscipline, helps to determine where the greatest damage falls. But the problems
faced by modern families are institutional in context. They
arise because old imperatives that held families together
have lost their force, and new supporting agencies and standards have not yet been developed to fill the gap. The preservation and strengthening of the family require more than
the attention of individuals to their family problems. They
require the strengthening of their individual capacities to
do so. And they also require organized social efforts to create
an environment that is congenial to the existence of stable
families.

This is a moment when the answer to any question is
likely to lie in a committee report or in the magic word "research." At the risk of announcing some premature findings,
without benefit of committee or prolonged research, I ven-
ture to suggest that some of the major factors behind family
problems are already well-known. They include inadequate
schools; crowded living conditions; ill health, physical and
mental; poverty; the steady pressures, humiliations, and
hostilities under which racial and ethnic minorities live;
the influence of a culture which makes much of technique
and little of ideas and purposes; and, not least, the unresolved paradoxes of a moral outlook which at one and the
same time connects sex with sin, uses sex to sell its products,
and teaches its young to regard a strong attraction for a
person of the opposite sex as something quasi-supernatural
which can conquer all and excuse all. Something has to give,
and what gives, in most cases, is the individual's belief that
he has been taught any standards by which he can live.

I do not expect that social workers or social statesmen
can produce a world in which all husbands are masterful

but flexible, all wives devoted but free and equal, all parents affectionate but not overly protective, all children happy but with developing minds of their own. Even if social workers and social statesmen had much more power than they now have—and much more wisdom—they could not produce such a world. It is well to recognize that when we turn to the family, we turn to the most intimate and precious area of ordinary human experience, and therefore the most perilous. And the perils are increased because our society places so high a value on individual freedom of choice and, therefore, so large a burden on individual powers of reason and self-discipline. Given all its inherent difficulties, however, the problem of forming and maintaining stable and vigorous families is immensely complicated by the failure to recognize that the social environment of modern families is different from that in which traditional families were sustained, and that organized and deliberate social efforts are required to provide new supports for the family.

It is also worth recognizing that such a program is not simply an effort to shore up an old institution against the tides beating upon it. It is an effort to achieve something singular and new. For the very changes which have made the family a more precarious institution have also given us a new and immensely elevated ideal of the family. In its perfected form, it is a free relationship between equals living together and sharing common enterprises for the delight they take in one another and in mutual devotion to the good. Aristotle spoke of an ideal form of friendship, and regarded it as the principal reward of the good life, second only to the practice of philosophy itself. The modern ideal of the family is the closest approximation we have to this ancient conception. Such an ideal, no doubt, can be achieved only rarely, but its dignity remains just the same. Just to keep that ideal alive will require an effort which will be immensely costly in money, work, and lost illusions. It seems to me to be worth the cost.

THE SCHOOL AND THE FAMILY

I. FROM THE VIEWPOINT OF
THE EDUCATOR

by *Robert J. Havighurst*

IN THE LONG PROCESS of social evolution, a number of social institutions were created by men to assist the basic institution of the family in making life satisfactory for human beings. The school is one of these institutions, and the welfare agency is another. Both of them appeared late on the scene, long after the institutions of religion, government, production, and commerce came into existence.

The more we learn about child-rearing, the more we are convinced that the family is all-important. We have learned that even an inadequate family is better for children than the best substitute we can invent. It is a very bad family indeed which is bad enough to cause our courts to take children from their parents and try to rear them in some other environment. The best substitute for a child's real family seems to be a foster family.

Nevertheless, the modern complex society has need of social institutions to supplement the family. These institutions—and especially the school and the family service agency—may assist the family with the personality, the character, and the intellectual development of its children.

Intellectual development is sometimes casually regarded as the function of the school, while personality and character development belong to the family. It is a serious mistake to look at things this way, for two reasons. First, human behavior is unified, so that the aspects we know as social behavior, moral behavior, and intellectual behavior are interrelated, and what affects one must affect the other two. Secondly, a seriously large group of families give their children a poor start in life to attain adult competence in social, moral, and intellectual behavior. The school *must* supplement these inadequate families.

All families must secure instruction for their children. Very few parents could teach their children the content of the school curriculum, even if they were able and willing to devote time to the task. All families also need access to a wholesome social group life for their children, such as may be provided by the school, church youth groups, Scouts, YMCA and YWCA, YMHA and YWHA, Camp Fire Girls, settlement houses, and so on.

Beyond this point, requirements vary enormously. In some instances, only minimal needs must be met outside a family's own resources. Other families can hardly care for any of the needs of their children without some sort of help.

We may assume that approximately half of the families in America can bring up their children quite nicely with the help given by the ordinary instructional program of the school, and with the youth organizations found in the average community. These are the families whose income is average or above average and whose heads have an average or more than average education. Of course, teachers and family service workers all know that there are inadequate families among those with above-average income and education. However, for our present purposes we shall ignore these exceptions, and consider that the families most in need of supplementary assistance are those whose family heads earn a below-average income and have received less than an average education.

The families under discussion may usefully be divided into two equal-sized groups. What might be called the "upper" working class, or the more prosperous and better educated half of the working class, do pretty well by their children. If the fathers and mothers in this group are asked what they want their children to obtain from the schools, they generally say, "a good sound education and some character training." If they are urged to state more specifically what kind of education they have in mind, they are likely to say, "I want my children to have more education than I got, and the kind of education that will help them get ahead in the world."

Here they express a desire for an educational supplement to the home which the people of above-average income and education do not need. They want a kind of intellectual stimulation, and they have a vision of what education might mean to their children that it has not meant to them.

These families of the upper working class also want public recreational facilities for their children—playgrounds, community centers, swimming pools, parks, and day camps. They need these things more than do families of higher socioeconomic status, who can generally pay for private facilities.

The need for intellectual stimulation, though not so acute, is similar to that of the "lower" working class.

The "lower" working class which comprises the quarter of the population whose income and education are in the lowest ranges, is mainly urban. Income is fairly good in time of full employment, but as many as a third to a half of its members are marginal workers. When unemployment reaches 5 or 6 percent of the total adult labor force, about half of the lower working class are likely to have unsteady employment. A considerable fraction of the group, in fact, spend more time receiving relief payments or unemployment compensation than they do working for steady wages.

Practically all the children in the lower working class are intellectually deprived, when compared with the children who come from families with better education and more income.

Jerry, a 10-year-old boy, is in the fifth grade. His father is a factory worker, and his mother keeps house for her husband and their four children. Jerry was slow in learning to read in the first grade; consequently, he was placed in a special class of nonreaders in the second grade, with an instructor selected for her ability to teach children who were having difficulty in learning. She had some assistance from a school social worker, a man, who visited the homes of the children and planned with her what to do about specific children.

They found that Jerry had an average IQ, and they gave him special attention in reading, which included frequent visits to the children's room of the public library. Jerry's reading quickly improved, and he took a liking to the library, where he went frequently after school. Later, he drew out books to read at home. Once he forgot to return a book when it was due, and his mother received a note from the librarian saying that the book was overdue and that Jerry had incurred a sixteen-cent fine. The mother returned the book but refused to pay the fine and told Jerry not to go to the library again. To her, a "fine" was a sign of lawbreaking, and she felt that neither she nor Jerry had broken a law.

When Jerry was in the fourth grade, the school social worker happened to meet him one afternoon after school in the neighbor-

hood of Jerry's home. They chatted a bit, and Jerry said that
he had a whole set of books at home, all his own. The worker
went home with him to see the books, and discovered a *Britannica
Junior* and a set of the *Book of Knowledge.* Jerry said that he
had read part of one of the books but it was too hard for him.
The worker asked whether anyone read to him, and Jerry said,
"No, Mom never reads them to me. She says I've got to do it
myself."

Jerry's mother came in at this time, and spoke cordially to
the worker, saying that she hoped to get Jerry's younger sister
into the first grade in September, though she would not be six
until December.

The worker commented later, "I thought it was interesting
that Jerry's parents would start payments on $280 worth of books
for the children, when these were the only books I saw in the
home; and that they would pay this money when they wouldn't
allow their son to go to the library because he owed a sixteen-cent
fine. I think they felt that the *Britannica* was a symbol of being
a good parent, and a symbol of prestige. And yet they did not
have the interest or the patience or the understanding to read
to Jerry, or to encourage him to use the public library."

When Jerry's experience is compared with the experience
of the average middle-class child with respect to books and
reading, it is clear that Jerry is suffering intellectual deprivation.

There is no evidence, however, that Jerry is emotionally
deprived. Gloria, a schoolmate of Jerry, did suffer from
emotional deprivation—lack of affection, lack of supervision,
and lack of consistent discipline.

Although she had an IQ of 98, Gloria at the age of 8 was
only reading in the first-grade reader, and was spending a second
year in the second grade. A shy, fearful, unkempt little girl, she
never spoke in class unless the teacher called on her, and then
she would often cry if the question was one she could not answer.
The teacher learned not to call on her for difficult work, and

began to give her a lot of affection. Noticing that Gloria sometimes came to school with face unwashed and hair uncombed, the
teacher one morning asked her what she had eaten for breakfast.
"Nothing," replied Gloria. "My mamma was in bed, and my
sister and me got up and came to school." The teacher sent her
to the school kitchen to get something to eat, and then took her
to the washroom and helped her wash herself. Coming back into
the class with her, the teacher held her close and commenced to
comb her hair. Gloria sat as quietly as though she was in a
trance, while the teacher worked with her hair and tied it up
in a "pony tail."

The next day, Gloria brought a note from her mother. "Dear
teacher," it read, "please leave her hair down like it was." At
this point the teacher visited Gloria's mother. The home con-
sisted of three rooms and a kitchen. Except for a television set,
the furniture in the living room would not bring two dollars
at an auction. There were dirty chairs and a dirty davenport,
and an old coal-burning stove with broken isinglass windows.
The mother complained about being a slave to her children. She
never had a good time anymore, she said. Now she was married
to a man who was better than her former husband who was "no
good, and went off and left me with four kids. This one is better
to the children; he is not so mean to them."

The mother went on, "If Gloria gives you any trouble, let me
know and I'll whip her. But leave her hair alone."

The teacher learned from this visit and from talking with
other people that Gloria's mother often went out for an evening
at a tavern, leaving her children to care for themselves. It was
probably after such an occasion that Gloria would come to
school unwashed and unfed the next morning. The teacher continued to pet Gloria, giving her more attention than she gave
to most of the other children. Gradually, the little girl came out
of her shell, while she was in the classroom. She would recite
freely, and by the end of the school year she had finished the
second reader and was ready for third grade. But she was still
very shy on the playground and sometimes came to school with
tear-stained face and uncombed hair. The school had supple-

mented the family, but was far from making up for the emotional deprivation suffered by the little girl.

There is fairly good evidence from several community studies that the lowest quarter of the population in terms of income and social status (with infrequent exceptions) fails to give its children adequate intellectual stimulation for success in school, and that as many as half of this group, or 12 percent of the total population, also fail to give their children adequate emotional support so that they will grow into competent adults.

Because the social pathology of unemployment, unstable families, illegitimate births, school failure, and juvenile delinquency is so highly concentrated in the slums of our cities and in the lower segment of the working class, we as a society turn to the teacher and the social worker and say: "You must do something about this situation."

What the school can do is to bring wholesome and effective influences to bear on children and their parents at certain strategic points in their lives. The school's influence seems to be most effective when youngsters are in kindergarten and the primary grades and when they are in the early teen-age years.

The most promising work of the schools has been done at the level of kindergarten and the primary grades. The teacher tries to make up for the emotional and intellectual deprivation suffered by the child in his family. Some of the best and most creative work with the children in our schools today is to be found in the kindergarten and primary grades of the slum schools, where teachers and social workers generally team together.

A number of large cities are trying out a type of program

that gives special assistance to the primary grades in the slum schools, on the theory that many of these children lack parental examples and stimulation to read and to achieve well in school. They fail to master the task of reading, and stumble along for the first few years in school, after which they become confirmed nonlearners, and social misfits during their adolescence. By putting specially trained teachers into relatively small classes, by using a social worker or visiting teacher to bring the home and school into contact, and by giving the children a variety of enrichment which middle-class children are more likely to get in their homes, we can give these children a better start in school and thus a better start in life.

A systematic attempt can be made to give lower-class children some of the intellectually stimulating experiences that are fairly common in middle-class families. The Higher Horizons program of New York City is an example. Through the school the children are given access to museums, libraries, theaters and concerts.

An interesting area of research just developing on the cognitive development of young children may suggest the extension of public schooling down to age three or four in lower-class districts, as a means of giving intellectual stimulation at a crucial point in the child's life. At this age, basic language patterns are learned which probably go a long way toward structuring the mind. Studies of the language used in lower- and in middle-class homes indicate that the typical lower-class home gives the child a language experience that is quite different from that in a typical middle-class home. The lower-class language patterns are simpler, with fewer qualifying adjectives and phrases, fewer complex sentences, fewer attempts to explain the meanings of words. If the research proves that lower-class children can be given a permanent boost of intelligence and of learning ability at the age of three or four, we shall see the development of public nursery schools with this aim.

Back of these attempts to make up for deprivation suffered by children of inadequate families stands the assumption that children of the lower working class are not born with any biological inferiority. However, if a child from any home is deprived of the intellectual stimulation or the emotional support to which he is biologically capable of responding, he will commence to fall behind in his mental and social development.

From what we now know of the mental and social development of children, and from what we know of the nature of family inadequacy, it is most important to spend society's money and effort on children as early as society can most effectively and efficiently supplement the family. Whether this age is three, four, or five years remains to be determined by research.

Improved development of young children will reduce the necessity to provide special attention for these children at older ages, but it will not eliminate this need. Probably a continued special program of intellectual enrichment and emotional support will be necessary throughout the school years. Meanwhile, there is a large group of boys and girls now in school, coming from inadequate families, who need whatever help can be given them, even though this help might better have been given when they were younger.

The last chance that the school has to do something for these children comes at the ages of thirteen, fourteen, and fifteen, or the junior high school age, just before they become old enough to quit school legally—and almost all of these boys and girls do quit school at sixteen or shortly afterward, if not before.

For boys of junior high school age there are a number of experimental work-study programs. Boys who, by the time they reach the seventh grade, show clear signs of social maladjustment and who do unsatisfactory schoolwork are being put into special classes which spend a part of the day in work experience of various kinds, while the rest of the school day is spent in an academic program adjusted to their learning abilities and interests. The work program may consist of socially valuable work on school and other community property, such as parks and playgrounds. Sooner or later, the work program evolves into part-time jobs with private employers. The aim is to help these boys to find an alternative pathway of growth to adulthood that is open to them if they try hard, since they have not been able to follow successfully the pathway of the academic school program.

Since boys of this type are frequently delinquent, they are easily recognized as a menace to society, and consequently the schools are asked to do something about them. However, their sisters are less visibly dangerous to society, since they seldom become aggressively delinquent. Nevertheless, the girls from inadequate homes are likely to do poorly in school and to drop out as soon as they can legally do so. Sometimes they leave at fourteen or fifteen because of pregnancy.

It is an established fact that girls from the lower working class families marry relatively early, frequently at ages sixteen to eighteen, and that these marriages often produce children who will repeat the vicious cycle in which their parents are caught. The schools might establish a program for these girls in their early teens which would attempt to help them become better wives and mothers, and to do a better job of rearing their children. For this kind of work, the teacher should also be a social group worker. This teacher would impart the skills and knowledge of caring for children and keeping a comfortable home. At the same time, she should organize the girls into a social group which will give them guidance and support in the developmental tasks of adolescent girlhood—getting ready for marriage and raising children, forming a scale of values that will help them to live socially responsible lives, and finding and marrying a satisfactory husband.

For something like 10 to 15 percent of our children, at least, the school must do as well as it can what the family has failed to do. This is a task for the joint efforts of schools and social agencies.

II. FROM THE VIEWPOINT OF

THE SOCIAL WORKER

by Bertram M. Beck

ONE DIFFICULTY OF ANALYZING the interrelationships between three such complex social institutions or systems as the school, social work, and the family is that all three are constantly changing internally as well as in relationship to one another. It is the nature of change and the way in which change is produced, however, which make this interrelationship important.

The changes which have taken place in the family over

the past fifty years have been exhaustively documented else-where.[1] Children are no longer an agrarian asset. They are a financial liability from birth through schooling. Father is not the head of an economic unit. Both parents may work. Economic aspirations promote mobility. Schooling, religion, recreation, medical care, and job placement are no longer functions of the family. Marriage is more frequent and somewhat earlier. We have more babies from more mar-riages, and each marriage tends to produce three or four children rather than one or two. Tasks are so shared be-tween men and women that a study in one community found that the only tasks specifically reserved to women were having babies and sewing. The family focus is on parents and chil-dren rather than on the family, children, kith and kin.

The facts are familiar. The supporting statistics deal with average families, so that amongst real families wide discrep-ancies are found, particularly when we view families from the vantage of class structure. The conclusions one can draw from such statistics can either be pessimistic or optimistic depending, I suspect, on the digestion of the concluder. Reuben Hill, attacking the Cassandras who see in divorce statistics signs of the demise of the family, points to the extraordinarily high incidence of marriage in this country. A divorce rate to be meaningful needs to be corrected by reference to the marriage rate just as a delinquency rate needs to be viewed in terms of the rising child population. Obviously, as chances of failure increase, the numbers of failures increase, but this truism is often ignored by the sensationalists. Viewing the divorce rate in the light of the

[1] Reuben Hill, "The American Family Today," in Eli Ginzberg, ed., *The Family and Social Change*, The Nation's Children, Vol. I (New York: Columbia University Press, 1960), pp. 76–107.

number of marriages contracted, we still have too many divorces. Since most divorced persons remarry one must assume that we are developing some system of trial marriages. The divorce rate is not, therefore, a problem to be dismissed, but neither should it be exaggerated.

Dr. Hill concludes that there is:

abundant proof that there is no repudiation of the basic business of families; namely, reproduction, housing, feeding, socializing, and guiding children from infancy to adulthood. Indeed, the family is now more of a specialized agency concentrating on personality development of its members, providing warmth, love, and sanctuary from the anonymity of urban existence, services no other agency in society is prepared to offer.[2]

Dr. Hill also says:

If greater stability of the family is ever to be assured, increasing the competence of young people in interpersonal relations and selecting people for marriage who are ready for parental responsibilities must be undertaken much more systematically.[3]

Such a program cannot be left to the family alone. In a psychological sense the sins of the father are indeed visited on the child. The youngsters who most need to achieve competence in interpersonal relations can least learn it from their parents. The youngsters who most need help in mate selection have the poorest models in their parents.

In a narrow sense, this means that education for family life as well as individual guidance should be found in the schools. In a broader sense, it means that the central focus of the school must be on equipping young people for a variety of crucial roles, including those involved in work, family, and play. Where the family fails, or is likely to fail,

[2] *Ibid.*, p. 84.   [3] *Ibid.*, pp. 99–100.

the school must do the job, for it is the logical social institution to take up the task.

The need to equip students for interpersonal relations does not apply with the same force in all instances. There must be some differential diagnosis to determine which youngsters are at greatest risk. Epidemiological studies of divorce have provided ample data concerning which ethnic, cultural, social, and economic factors are associated with divorce and marital incompatibility.[4] If we can have a four-track curriculum for youngsters with varying intellectual endowment, why should we not have a different curriculum for youngsters with differing social, cultural, emotional, and intellectual endowment?

I would not for a moment propose anything so crude as classes for the emotionally handicapped since I would doubt their value and fear the consequences of the stigma. I am suggesting a four-, five-, or six-track curriculum with each track designed to meet a certain constellation of unmet needs. For those youngsters whose major unmet needs were intellectual, the major fare would be academic. The gifted child, however, whose future capacity as a parent was in doubt because of certain needs unmet in his own family would not be fed on science and mathematics alone. In a similar fashion, children who because of social factors were lacking in academic motivation could be aided to overcome the handicaps of their home environment. It was to these children that I made reference when I noted that statistics regarding the family give a picture of most families, not those whose pattern is distorted by social exile.

[4] Jessie Bernard, "Neomarital Programs," in *The Social Welfare Forum, 1958* (New York: Columbia University Press, 1958), pp. 239–68.

Twenty years ago Dr. Havighurst and Dr. Davis made their ground-breaking study revealing the impact of class on learning.[5] More recently, James B. Conant has taught us the lesson *"that to a considerable degree what a school should do and can do is determined by the status and ambition of the families being served."* [6] Conant describes schooling in certain urban Northern slums. He finds that these slums are largely inhabited by Negroes who have recently moved from the South seeking to better themselves. Victims of discrimination—North or South—these parents have had limited educational opportunity and obviously provide their children with a great deal less cultural and educational stimulation than do more favored families— Negro and white. The social sins visited on the fathers are visited on the sons. The youngsters have little reason to believe that vertical mobility up the ladder of prestige and power is a real possibility. Lacking motivation for self-denial they tend to grab immediate satisfactions. This means truancy, school drop-out, unemployment, and possibly delinquency.

These youngsters obviously need more than good education. They need special education along the lines of the Higher Horizons program in New York [7] aimed at motivating slum children who can achieve to achieve; or the Bannekev program in St. Louis where amazing progress was

[5] Allison Davis and Robert J. Havighurst, "Social Class and Color Differences in Child-Rearing," in Guy E. Swanson *et al.*, eds., *Readings in Social Psychology* (rev. ed., New York: Henry Holt and Co., 1952), p. 550.

[6] James Bryant Conant, *Slums and Suburbs* (New York: McGraw-Hill, 1961), p. 1.

[7] Daniel Schreiber, "Higher Horizons," *American Child*, XLIII, No. 2 (1961), 12.

made with enriched opportunities for nineteen schools in a depressed area.[8]

Varying opportunities for different constellations of intellectual, emotional, and social needs in one school demand a school with a heterogeneous population. Conant recommends such a school for rural areas and smaller cities but regretfully believes that in the suburban and urban area we must live with *de facto* segregation.[9]

Whatever may be the present problems in planning for the future we must promote a form of regional and neighborhood planning that does not segregate by color, class, or economics. In schools serving such neighborhoods there could be differential understanding and differential curriculum.

Although I have drawn an analogy to "tracking" as it is now used in some school systems I am not thinking of the mechanical expedient of putting children into fixed groups. I am proposing the use of specialists by the school for regular appraisal of children's needs and a varied curriculum to meet these different needs.

In retrospect, one of the evils of the misapplication of the principles usually associated with "progressive education" was often the exposure of all youngsters to some corrective "life adjustment" experience which ignored the varying abilities of families to prepare for different roles. Cold War fears have led to the charge that some schools are so concerned with "adjustment" that they are not educating, and around this banner various misguided persons flock.

[8] Conant, *op. cit.*, p. 62.
[9] James Bryant Conant, *The American High School Today* (New York: McGraw-Hill, 1959).

Actually, academic progress is closely associated with mental health, so there is nothing contradictory about concern with academic achievement and with mental health.[10] Reasonable objections to waste of intellectual abilities and interests can be met, however, by differential understanding and curriculum.

Except by happenstance or therapeutic intervention the family which is failing in respect to its functions cannot change itself. Therefore, the school must change in order more successfully to intervene in the life of the youngsters whose parents fail, in order to prepare the youngsters to be successful parents themselves.

Social work's role is to make the maximum contribution to inducing this change in the schools. Social work is often envious of education because of the public interest and support that the schools attract. The interest is not an unmixed blessing, however, since every special-interest group in the country has some ax to grind in the public school system. Social work should not overestimate its uniqueness or its power potential under such circumstances. Nevertheless, the profession cannot overlook its responsibility to formulate policy and carry it forward.

The social work profession has little social policy that is problem-oriented. If one examines the National Association of Social Workers statement on public education one finds it is essentially a statement that could just as well be issued by the National Education Association.[11] There is little definition of social work's contribution to the attainment of

[10] Lorene A. Stringer, "Academic Progress as an Index of Mental Health," *Journal of Social Issues*, XV, No. 1 (1959), 16.

[11] *Goals of Public Social Policy* (New York: National Association of Social Workers, 1959), p. 27.

educational goals. There has been no such definition because the concept of that contribution has largely been
limited to casework service within the school system.

Up until the last five years this approach by social work
to problems through method rather than through knowledge has characterized the profession. Because so much attention had been absorbed by the development and teaching
of casework method based largely on psychoanalytical theory,
social workers tended to see solutions to problems in terms
of what the social worker could do rather than in terms of
what was demanded. The problem of family breakdown, for
example, would elicit the solution of family casework. If the
schools were involved at all it would be through the school
social worker's offering casework help to the child and family in the interest of enhancing the child's performance as
a pupil.

This approach has several major limitations. Firstly, the
incidence of breakdown is so great and the shortage of
therapeutic personnel so appalling that if we are to depend
exclusively on individualized help we might as well give up
now. Secondly, psychologically oriented individual treatment seems least helpful for those families who need it most
—the socially disadvantaged groups with which Conant was
concerned. Not only is it extremely difficult to help these
families in this manner, but even if the social worker can
help, a new family sickens for each one cured since the roots
of the disease are not psychological.

Recently, the profession has been concerned with viewing
problems from the vantage point of values and knowledge
—separating what we believe and what we know from what
we, or anybody else, can do. When we apply such an approach to the problem of how the school can prevent family

breakdown there is developed the formulation I have presented, although it is undoubtedly only one of many possible social inventions to meet the situation. It is of significance, however, that it focuses on a mass program to aid discriminant groups of young people. It puts the priority on prevention of family malfunction in the next generation even though, ideally, we would want to aid the existing family also, if we could. It sees the social worker in the schools as mainly engaged in assessing needs and helping with pupil placement to meet needs rather than in offering individual therapeutic service either through casework or consultation. It by no means rules out individual treatment, but that is not viewed as the major focus.

Social work cannot look to school social workers as the major vehicle for inducing change in the schools. Ideally, social work looks to its practitioners in a field such as the schools to make "a contribution to the character and goals of the institution." [12] There is no doubt that social workers who have practiced in schools have done this, but, to my knowledge, the underlying reasons for the slow development of social work in the schools remains unexplored. School social work is about as old as medical social work.[13] The opportunities for expansion of social work in the schools are far greater than the opportunities in hospitals and health facilities. The problem of gaining acceptance from medicine is certainly as great as gaining acceptance from education. Yet the medical social workers are far ahead in numbers, resources, standards, and recognition. Why?

[12] Subcommittee on Fields of Practice, "Identifying Fields of Practice," *Social Work*, VII, No. 4 (1962), 7.

[13] John C. Kidneigh, "Social Work as a Profession," in Russell H. Kurtz, ed., *Social Work Year Book, 1960* (New York: National Association of Social Workers, 1960), p. 568.

For want of a better explanation I suggest two reasons. First, education is too close to social work in its purposes, the values to which it subscribes, and the knowledge it commands readily to recognize social work as a separate profession with a special contribution. The tendency is to see social work as an interloper and a competitor. This is aggravated by the fact that both social work and education are relatively young professions. Their status positions are not far apart. The salaries are similar. The class, culture, and motivations of persons recruited to these professions are the same. Both groups are employees in bureaucratic structures. Medicine would hardly view social work as a competitor for a place in the sun. It would, however, be quite reasonable for education to see social work as competition for professional status. This might explain why out of education there has developed a variety of pupil personnel services with functions similar to, or identical with, those of the school social worker and the school psychologist. For these reasons the use of social workers within the school is but one means by which social work can induce change in the school toward enhancement of family function.

Equally important is social action by the profession to support the growth and development of our school systems. Legislative priorities in the professional associations' lobbying tend to be assigned to programs in which social workers are heavily involved. Of greater import in setting such priorities is the significance of the measure in terms of achieving social work purposes. Viewed in this perspective the schools are the first order of business.

Social workers can also contribute to improvement of school programs in their positions as staff members of civic and planning organizations. This is differentiated from lobbying in so far as the social worker in the professional practice of community organization is not the ardent advocate of a particular solution. He does, however, help the committees and groups with which he works to define problems and seek solutions. The community organization worker who himself sees the potential of the school can aid others in lending creative support to needed development.

Lastly, social workers can help by the development of adjunctive social work services which would be physically within the school but administratively adjacent to it. One must beware of following the medical or psychiatric model in respect to schools because of the significant differences in the so-called "host" profession. Under the plan I am suggesting, the administrator of the adjunctive services would not be responsible to the principal but might be responsible to an associate superintendent concerned with health and welfare services. The adjunctive social work program would be distinguished from the program of school social work inasmuch as the latter would be sharply focused on aiding the school in the discharge of its educational functions.

Elsewhere I have described the range and function of the adjunctive services.[14] They are essentially designed to enhance, restore, and maintain family function. They would be located at the school because the school offers natural entree into the life of so many families. The program would include opportunities for family recreation and education usually associated with settlements and community centers. Day care facilities for children of working mothers would also be available, as would be employment and guidance services for out-of-school, out-of-work youth and adults. The public assistance and social insurance programs would have offices there, as would the probation service of the juvenile

[14] Bertram M. Beck, "Children on the New Frontier," *Child Welfare,* XL, No. 4 (1961), 1–5.

and adult court. In so far as individual casework and psychotherapy were available these facilities would be found in the center. From the adjunctive service center would radiate detached workers for approach to hostile youth groups unrelated to center activities and also neighborhood workers to stimulate local activities for community improvement.

This utopian conception is born of the recognition that social work services do not reach those most in need because the services are structured and offered in a way that defeats this purpose. The design proposed has the merit of bringing the preventive in close proximity to the curative so as to remove the stigma from the curative. It places service on a neighborhood level in relationship to a basic social institution—the school. Simplicity, economy, and efficiency are achieved by putting all basic programs and services under one roof rather than developing overlapping, yet functionally unrelated, islands of service each under the banner of a different problem but all utilizing the same approach.

In order to achieve any semblance of such reorganization enormous resistance to change within the social work profession would have to be overcome. The chain, therefore, completes itself. To change the school so that it can produce certain changes in certain families, social work must change itself. This, then, is the first order of business for social work. In the past we have lacked power to induce change in our own profession because there was no organization for formulation of the profession's point of view as opposed to the point of view of agencies and organizations. Today we have our own organization and at least a power potential. To challenge the best that is within us, therefore, it is well that we dream with imagination so that tomorrow's reality can come closer to the heart's desire.

PUBLIC WELFARE SERVICES AND FAMILY LIFE

by Norman V. Lourie

THERE IS A NEW ATMOSPHERE around public welfare. It holds promise for improving social services to families and children. But we are still far from a new day, a basic change in basic values, or possession of all the tools and methods that we need if we are to eliminate the welfare gaps.

We are agreed that social welfare, including public welfare services, is essential in a democratic society.

Strong family life and maximum family stability are considered important values in America. Public welfare services are expected to help assure that every family has the essentials to promote these values. They have made great contributions. There has been tremendous advance, but there are also gaps.

It would be oversimplification and an untruth to suggest that the provision of complete public welfare programs would reflect the values of all Americans. More accurately, the values of many, based on life experiences, local histories, sentiments, and emotions, are at variance with those which might be derived from the cold facts of our capacity to improve and foster strong family stability.

The system of public welfare stems from the concept that each individual and family is of intrinsic worth. This is a corollary of our constitutional guarantees set out in the Bill of Rights.

On this concept we based public specialized programs to solve particular problems and to meet particular needs.

Another corollary to the concept of intrinsic worth provides that, when necessary, individual and family should be buffered by government from the assaults of disease and deprivation both social and economic.

For these purposes we devised many therapeutic and protective programs.

There seems to be general agreement on the principle of intrinsic worth. There must be at least majority agreement on the corollaries or else the program would not exist at all.

There is not general agreement on the belief that all individuals and families should have the best opportunity for full growth and development in line with current knowledge. Nor is there general agreement that they should have protections consonant with up-to-date knowledge of how to provide effective protections.

This is where the value system becomes important. How much are we willing to tax or be taxed for public welfare services to families and children? What level of deprivation can we tolerate with comfort? What are the priorities in serving the general welfare? Must we tolerate poverty in the midst of plenty in order to provide a sound definition of the American way? Do certain aspects of economic development need to precede the development of human welfare? Are incomplete welfare programs a price to be paid for defense?

These are not easy choices. They point up the paradoxes. For example:

1. We ruled out infant and maternal death rates on a

large scale, but our meager public assistance grants and Social Security benefits deny decent housing and enough food, clothing, and family comfort for millions.

2. We ruled out death from starvation, but we do not provide adequate care for the chronically disabled.

3. We ruled out as inhumane confinement of the mentally ill in the almshouse, but not lifetime confinement in a mental hospital because we cannot afford the intensive treatment that might secure release and return to society.

4. We ruled out forcing families to break up for unnecessary reasons, yet we refuse to train enough professional manpower to provide the personal helping services needed to keep families intact.

5. We delayed death to the eighth decade, but we maintain an economy which pushes out the older worker and denies him the means to maintain health and self-respect in retirement.

6. We ruled out ignorance and idleness, yet we allow millions of young people to drop out of high school into an empty labor market. We are as yet unwilling to provide adequate public support for education and vocational training.

7. We glut our storage bins with agricultural surpluses, yet we permit exploitation of thousands of migrant families who live in squalor and under circumstances which preclude stable family life.

8. We encourage the one-generation family, but we impose heart-rending codes of relatives' responsibility.

9. We glorify family stability, but we administer support laws in ways that discourage reunion of broken families.

We need agreement that, to develop real independence in the democratic spirit, dependency needs must first be met humanely and equitably, and all services required to assure full development and family stability shall be available to all people.

The financial underpinning for the American family needs a major overhauling. The levels of all grants and benefits must be increased to minimums of health and decency. A family allowance system should be considered. The social insurances should be improved and extended to provide flexible benefits consistent with the cost of living and should include comprehensive health care.

Public welfare alone cannot fill the gaps in the economic system. Improvements in other social and economic programs, including education, manpower training, housing, urban redevelopment, industrial development, and public works, are essential if public welfare services are to be effective.

Vast unmet needs exist for all family and children's services and will increase as the population grows.

Professional services are in short supply. There is no major relief in sight. We must train more professional workers. We also must make more creative and productive use of untrained personnel.

There is great confusion, conflict, and duplication among the many public and voluntary agencies that offer services. We have no means to measure the effectiveness of our total effort. We are hard pressed to make reasoned decisions about an improved structure.

Despite the increased funds spent by public and voluntary agencies there is little assurance that expenditures are directed to priority needs.

Finally, any substantial improvement in services to families and children must proceed on three fronts: a basic change in national values as reflected in legislation and public policy; extension and improvement of public welfare services; unqualified support of public welfare programs by the voluntary sector.

The new atmosphere reflects all three. In the backwash of Newburgh the reaction of news media, while critical of public welfare's failings, recognized the need for professional services and a change in orientation. Our national leadership has spoken out vigorously for change, and has proposed new Federal legislation and new approaches to public welfare programming by the Department of Health, Education, and Welfare. There is solid support of all these by the voluntary field.

For the first time in history a President of the United States delivered a message on welfare to the Congress. In his address President John F. Kennedy said: "The times, the conditions, the problems have changed—and the nature and objectives of our public assistance and child welfare programs must be changed also, if they are to meet our human needs."

The President told Congress that communities which attempted to save money on welfare expenditures through ruthless and arbitrary cutbacks met with little success. "But communities which have tried the rehabilitative road—the road I recommended today—have demonstrated what can be done with creative, thoughtfully conceived and properly managed programs of prevention and social rehabilitation."

In his testimony on H.R. 10606, designed to amend the Social Security Act, Abraham Ribicoff, then Secretary of Health, Education, and Welfare, included these objectives of the new approach: services to help families become self-supporting and independent; prevention of dependency by dealing with problems that cause it; incentives to recipients to improve their conditions and to the states to improve their programs; services to rehabilitate clients or those likely to become clients; training in order to increase the supply of adequately prepared public welfare personnel. He talked about a new spirit in public welfare programs and said: "We now have an historic and constructive opportunity to reinforce these programs—to bring them up to date—and so to benefit our nation and all of its people."

This testimony, the House Ways and Means Committee report on H.R. 10606, and other related documents are historic. They should be studied carefully. With the President's statement they represent a shift in national policy thinking and support values consistent with objectives that the public welfare field has long held.

A series of administrative directives issued by the Secretary represent a strong commitment to alter public welfare operations in order to improve services to families and children. The tone of national leadership is new. With enactment of H.R. 10606, sometimes called the "Welfare Improvements bill," law, policy, and money will be used to bring about fundamental changes in the emphasis of state and local programs and to promote broader coverage. The proposed public welfare amendments are probably the most significant from the social services standpoint since the Social Security Act was passed in 1935.

One of the issues brought up in consideration of H.R. 10606 was concerned with purchase of service from voluntary agencies that use public assistance funds. This provision was removed from the bill by the House and not requested of the Senate by the Secretary. It was opposed by many, including some voluntary agencies. Some suggested limitations on purchase to prevent a voluntary agency from deriving too large a portion of its budget from public funds.

Services to be purchased are not specified in the bill. Apparently, casework, counseling, and other social services are meant—services which are generally not available in public welfare agencies; services which are rehabilitative in nature and essential to the reorientation of the public welfare program. Oddly enough, the bill refers to services purchased by other public agencies from nonprofit agencies and makes specific provision for public welfare agencies to pay the other public agency for these services.

Purchase of voluntary services by public welfare agencies is not new. Public welfare buys large amounts of varied health services and child welfare services. The important question is not simply what should be our policy about purchase (although that question needs to be resolved). Rather we must decide what brand of public agency we want. The other answers will follow from this decision.

When public agencies achieve a reasonable degree of quality in their own services to families and children and exercise their responsibility to assure coverage, there will be a better atmosphere in which to work out the public-voluntary relationships. In too many communities the public agency has not fulfilled its basic responsibility.

We should ultimately address ourselves to creating a welfare system in which social services are given to families and children without the requirement that for those on public assistance (the last group), the service must be tied to financial need. Financial aid and social services can be offered by the same agency, but each can exist for its own worth.

Not much noticed in H.R. 10606 is the new provision that services can be given to applicants for assistance as well as to persons who have been or are likely to become recipients. This too has great potential for changing the public welfare agency into a family service center. Public welfare will need a great deal of help to get ready for this job.

There are inconsistencies in public policy with respect to eligibility for service. Some public services, although insufficient in quantity, are usually available without reference to the applicant's financial status (although ability to pay may be taken into consideration in setting fees): mental hospitals and clinics; maternal and child health; employment service; vocational rehabilitation; public health nursing; child welfare; care for the tuberculous and the mentally retarded, and so on.

Now for the first time (except for medical care), Federal support will be available for a wide range of social services both to assistance and some nonassistance clients. This, together with the new urgency better to coordinate child welfare and public assistance, provides the real basis for the development of broad-gauged public family and children's agencies.

Previously, I have identified seven requirements that must be fulfilled if we are to achieve a more appropriate and effective structuring of services for preventive and therapeutic action, for a proper framework within which our rehabilitative efforts can have maximum results. I continue to believe that they are sound:

1. Uniform definitions of the problems of families and individuals that are universally understandable and can be operationally applied
2. Testing of the concept of problem-solving as contrasted with the open-end provision of services
3. A workable and uniformly applied definition of the concepts of prevention

4. A framework for comprehensive diagnosis as a basis for differential treatment

5. Development of criteria for the community-wide allocation of responsibility and services

6. Development and use of systems of constant evaluation and accountability

7. Creation of real leadership with the freedom to operate.

The final point is one of critical importance. Present leadership is divided among the many national and local groups which promote improvement of their own services to deal with various specific problems.

We are still uncertain about the degree of competence needed to handle different aspects of maladjustment. I know of no community plan that clearly defines and coordinates organizational responsibility, that directs the stream of applicants among the several systems of service.

Questions of structure and division of responsibility are far from solution. Our present patterns will find many families and children falling between seats to a hard floor.

The rehabilitative process is not the function of any one agency. The life process itself proceeds in a series of phases, and the welfare system must be adequate to handle issues as and where they arise. Services must be organized to allow for a continuum of efforts ranging from early prevention to maximum rehabilitation. Machinery and agencies are created by man; if he desires, man can integrate them to meet his objective.

Assuming that we have met the seven requirements, and assuming the acceptance of a common philosophy about the rehabilitative role, what may we expect?

The agencies in any community could, together, possess uniform information about the incidence of known problems and needs. They might, on an ongoing basis, be able to understand more completely the families and children who need help. And there would be a better basis for engineering the flow of cases into proper channels for service. This would be a very advanced stage in public welfare. I believe that our ultimate goal will not be achieved until we have reached it.

For instance, we know that there are severe personnel problems in all programs. I am not certain that we can know what quality and quantity of personnel we really need until we have a more accurate measure of the needs that the clientele present.

We do not have effective methods by which to evaluate the results of our services to families and children. Our methods are as yet fragmentary and dissimilar. Often we resist true evaluation. Consequently, our accountability to the supporting public is based on generalities. Perhaps we will be able to gauge success and failure by reflecting accepted criteria of problems against prevalence and incidence rates and the movement of cases in and out of our various agencies and systems of agencies.

This does not mean that we do not have evidence of successful cases. These are usually accounted for by each agency alone, on its own standards of judgment and its specialized objectives.

Yes, we do have a new opportunity to reorient our efforts in behalf of families and children. I hope we can take it. National policy, new public welfare legislation and directives, wholehearted support of the profession, concerned citizens, and voluntary social agencies are on the move.

For us there has always been a new frontier.

HOUSING DESIGN, NEIGHBORHOOD PLAN, AND FAMILY LIFE

by Elizabeth Wood

WE REALLY DO NOT KNOW HOW to design houses and neighborhoods so that they will have the most creative impact on family life. By "we," I mean planners, architects, critics and students of the subject, including sociologists. We have unsystematic and sometimes inaccurate reporting; we have some feminine intuitions and architectural insights; we have a handful of fragmentary sociological studies. We do not have knowledge. Instead, we have stereotypes about slums, their inhabitants, their housing needs, and their social characteristics. We have old stereotypes and we have new stereotypes.

In the area of urban renewal, a fundamental working knowledge is in the process of being acquired *today*. The course of its development will depend on the degree to which the social work profession recognizes and participates in this acquisition of knowledge through action.

We can congratulate ourselves that at long last the information that urban renewal deals with people as well as with bricks and mortar has become a cliché. The administrators, architects, planners, building managers, and city officials all know it. Although they do not know how to turn the cliché into urban design, they are trying with a quality of sensitivity and urgency that is to be respected. They have to, whether they like it or not, because human frailties, problem people, and the products of bad urban design do not indefinitely remain concealed when urban renewal begins to be effective.

Their sense of urgency—if not guilt—has been greatly increased during the last year by the emergence of a new school of thought and many confusing recommendations as to how they should run their operations. This new school finds that slums are not what they were once supposed to be.

Thirty years ago, everybody—planners, engineers, sociologists, and mayors—knew what a slum was and could identify it by means of well-established statistical tests. They all knew that a slum was bad, and that it was good to tear it down. The new school of thought believes that slums "provide many sources of residential satisfaction," that they have social structure, neighborliness, safety, and many other "positive factors." It finds that it is good to have children playing on the streets in front of stoops; a mixture of neighborhood shops and houses is good; "bad" buildings are not necessarily bad; pubs are good; parks and playgrounds are not necessarily good; good social structure is good even if the buildings are bad; the lack of social structure is bad even if the buildings are good. In addition, they find numerous bad things in the housing projects that were designed in accordance with what were formerly accepted as good social principles.

All this is very confusing, but it is also very useful. I hope that one of the results of the confusion will be the launching of a great number of studies by those whose occupation is study and research rather than operation and reporting. We need a great many of the slow, detailed, infinitely laborious but necessary pieces of academic research.

The confusion and the criticism have also been useful because they have highlighted for urban renewal administrators the necessity of doing something different. And they *are* so doing. Most cities have initiated rehabilitation projects and are emphasizing this program instead of clearance and rebuilding—the bulldozer program. This means that urban renewal agencies are repairing and remodeling as many buildings as possible, demolishing only the hopeless buildings, and raising the quality of amenities through public improvements, such as schools, playgrounds, and so forth.

Unlike clearance programs, rehabilitation in a substandard area deals with people and buildings *as they are* and *where they are*. Thus the urban renewal agency cannot operate in its accustomed manner. It deals with a piece of the city in which there are the usual social and economic indices of blight, although the percentage may not be so high as that in clearance areas. Frequently, it must also deal with the toughest of city problems—the race problem in a changing neighborhood.

Since, by definition, the program requires the active participation of both landlords and tenants, the basic tool is community organization. Up to now, community organization has been regarded as part of the social work profession. Yet, some of the best community organization work I have seen—in Dayton and in Boston—is being done by men who never saw even the outside of a school of social work.

The object of community organization is to get the people to plan for themselves. It is in this process, when people lay out their own homes and neighborhoods, that we have the maximum opportunity to learn about urban design. What we learn, however, is not a group of architectural principles, that high buildings are good or not good, and low ones are the opposite. We learn something about the people's desire for and capacity to use what architects and planners hitherto have thought was best. Not all people want something different from what they have. Nor do they all want to plan. The job is to stimulate people to aspire to the limits of their capacity and to help them fulfill their aspirations. The job is also to define for the urban renewal agency the limits of the aspirations of some people; to explain the fact that, in any one neighborhood, one cannot persuade all the people to want what they should want; and that some of the things they want are not what professional planners think are good and proper.

It has seemed to me very often that in order to find out how to help people to aspire, to plan, we need to take a lesson from that oldest of workers in the field, that old lady "the City." For years, working in real and mystical ways, she has been raising people's aspirations and capacities. She has taken to her bosom—the slums—the newcomers, the poor, the ignorant. In due time, as their incomes increased, they began to move into successively better neighborhoods, adopting better standards as they came into contact with progressively more urbanized families. The process has taken a generation or two, and often neighborhoods slipped down in the process, because there has always been a precipitation of the less adaptable, the less aspiring, along the route. The process has a name—the urbanizing process.

Our knowledge of how it works is far from precise. We

know that cities are concentrations of jobs, of cultural and educational institutions, of the moneyed, the best dressed. As such, they have served as the generators of the standards and aspirations of the whole country. We know that families at every stage of the urbanizing process are in direct and indirect contact with these things. Their aspirations are stimulated; they are driven to fulfill their ambitions. We do not know just how this happens, but not to be underestimated is the impact of neighbor on neighbor; the impact of schools, newspapers, shop windows, advertisements, and TV commercials.

The earlier public housing programs sought, by changing the housing factor, to expedite the urbanizing process. When this did not succeed automatically with all people —though it always has for some—we sought the help of social services.

The rehabilitation program endeavors to expedite the urbanizing process in another way. It starts with people where they are, physically and socially. It brings to bear a complex system of education to help people plan for themselves in their own home and their own neighborhood.

Since the different sections of the city contain different mixes of people at different stages of the climb, the quality of aspirations, the level of achievement, and, therefore, the character of their design for living will differ in each section. If we are responsive to this fact, our knowledge of urban design will put an end to the stereotypes that confuse everybody today.

A rehabilitation program includes several technical operations, all of which use the community organization tool. These include: planning; code enforcement; promotional work to stimulate owners to repair and beautify their properties and technical service to help them to do it. Technical staff, located in a field office, provide property owners with information concerning what can be done for each building; sketches of what the remodeled building will look like; and the estimated cost of doing it. Staff will help work out the economics of the remodeling—the amount of the monthly mortgage payments, the way in which rents will be affected—and will help locate mortgage money.

Each of these activities can, and in some cities does, perform an effective educational function by expediting the urbanizing process. But they are not always used thus. Some function purely mechanically. Local redevelopment administrators and their associates do not always see all the ways in which these activities can serve the educational, the urbanizing process.

Take the planning operation. The theory is that the people will plan their neighborhoods within such framework as the planners give them. This is where motivation begins, where one seeks to touch and raise aspirations. One of the tools used in Boston for this purpose is a questionnaire directed at getting the people to identify or realize the deficiencies in their neighborhood. The questions cover such things as schools, parks, traffic, traffic lights, condition of streets, garbage collection. These questionnaires are discussed in small meetings of neighbors. It is not difficult to arouse concern over deficiencies that are the fault of others. The channeling of the aroused energy into political action and self-help programs demands skilled leadership.

But it is not only skilled leadership that is needed. The city departments too must be geared to deliver contributions to the community program: the new school, park, traffic light, better garbage collection. There is no stimulant so effective as a little success.

Code enforcement is essential in rehabilitation. It is, technically, the only legal tool that can be used in bringing buildings up to the city's minimum standards. The fact that it is a *legal* tool is important in the design of a socially oriented program; not because it provides police power for enforcement, but because it offers the only legal means of entrance to every building and dwelling unit in a rehabilitation area.

What an inspector does, depends on what kind of a man he is and what kind of a program he is a part of. In Dayton, the code enforcement inspectors were quite special in their deep human concern, their insights, their resourcefulness. They were expert case-finders. Whenever possible, they called upon available resources and helped needy cases. They raised loud voices to try to get necessary services for those they could not help. Due to the excellent work of the professional community organization worker, the local resources were the businessmen and the churches. In one neighborhood were several old people who owned their own homes, which they could not bear to leave, whose income was solely from Social Security payments, and who could not conceivably raise the $1,500 or $1,800 necessary to bring their homes up to legal standards. In one instance, the inspector scrounged around until he found the required plumbing fixtures, which were donated by the contractor who was demolishing at a near-by clearance site. He then persuaded the plumbing contractor in the businessmen's group to install them free. In another case, the inspector obtained secondhand gutters and downspouts and asked the man in the sheet-metal business to install them. The man said he would not fool with the secondhand stuff, and he installed new ones, free. One of the churches sponsored weekend work camps for teen-agers. The campers tore down the old people's back sheds, cleaned up yards, painted houses.

Take the program of building repair and remodeling. In the usual program, the local redevelopment agency sets up a field office staff; distributes a quantity of promotional leaflets that show how to make repairs of all kinds; conducts some demonstrations; and meets evenings with homeowners to show them slides of Before and After. At this point, the operation touches the very wellspring of a family's hopes—and also comes face to face with the realities of living in a blighted area. Here, the design for living is constructed by the grass roots for the grass roots. The product will not be like that proposed by graduates of architectural schools, who see results in terms of Le Corbusier, Gropius, Sert.

The field architectural staff suffer when a homeowner, responding enthusiastically to their promotional efforts, paints his house pink to match the magnificent pink Lincoln that stands in front. They suffer over the design prototypes that they must prepare for the remodeling of the architectural monstrosities in their areas: the three-deckers of Boston; the high, narrow-gabled boxes of other cities. The ugliness of these buildings seems invulnerable. The homeowners' sense of beauty is scarcely that of the field staff. The architects ask themselves, "So what do you have when you finish a 'rehab' job?"

I cannot refrain from adding that I wish that there were greater use in rehabilitation programs of that oldest device for covering up architectural mistakes—vines, bushes, and trees.

The conflict between planners and the needs of people in the early stages of the urbanizing process arises over other matters, such as the mixture of business and homes. "Good" neighborhoods forbid the methods of increasing incomes that are necessary in these early stages: taking in roomers; running a little radio repair shop, delicatessen, or a cleaning shop in basement or garage; doing dressmaking or hairdressing in the home. Such enterprises are especially frowned upon if there is a sign in the window.

Sometimes when we are confronted with the worst possible conditions and there are no restrictions on the solutions, we can think straight to need and design. It is a wonderful exercise. I had the chance in India.

The basic goal of the Calcutta Metropolitan Planning Organization, to which I am consultant, is the preparation of an economic development program. One task was to design a *bustee* redevelopment scheme. A *bustee* is an urban hut slum.

Indian legislation requires that relocation housing must be erected before substandard units can be torn down. One has, therefore, the opportunity to plan for particular *bustee* people. One begins by studying them.

The Indian policy, like ours, is to ignore business relocation. Displaced businesses died or moved into already crowded adjacent bustees.

Now, the Maniktala bustee had hundreds of little businesses. There were shops, 4 x 8 feet, where food or clothing was sold. There were shops where the whole family, from grandmother to five-year-old, sat on the floor and smacked beads with a hammer on a stone to make sequins. There were bangle-makers, whose equipment was a big stone, a little rubbing stone, and a basket of sliced conch shells. There were tailors whose equipment was a sewing machine. There were a few larger businesses, occupying a hut or even two.

Our solution was based on the thesis that little business-men were too important to India to be killed off; that relocation and rehousing must bring about their strengthening and expansion wherever possible; that physical design must reflect the economic realities of these little businesses: that they used all the members of the family; that they needed tiny bits of space; that they could not pay separate rents for business and shelter. It was also based on a long-term program of education, service, and expansion after relocation. This was possible because of the type of service available from the West Bengal Department of Small Industries.

The resultant design is a compound, a complex of work space and shelter. We will, for example, relocate all the little tailors in one area, so that over the years the Department can introduce new production methods. Meanwhile, the Department will develop cooperative programs for securing and delivering raw materials, for merchandising, for accounting.

Several points are worth mentioning:

1. This plan represents concepts unacceptable to almost every architect, engineer, and building manager, and to all administrators of all the Federal, state, and local agencies responsible for carrying out urban renewal plans.

2. It is right, in that it fits perfectly the needs and capacities of the people for whom it is intended.

3. Its design, and the analysis preceding the design, involved not only the architect, but an anthropologist, a couple of sociologists, and economists.

4. To a certain degree, the design can be adjusted to fit the needs of the people as their incomes and their aspirations expand.

5. The management staff is dedicated to a program of this kind of expansion.

Fortunately, in our own metropolitan areas we do not have to deal with such a low level of economy. But there are, I believe, some lessons for us in the process and the story.

Let me repeat my beginning statement: The most dynamic program for raising the social and economic level of the families in our slums and blighted areas is now going on under the direction of the men who are engaged in urban renewal. Never has social work had so many allies.

Yet, social workers are worried to death about the implications for their operations of this huge case-finding undertaking. I know exactly why. Agency budgets are too small; personnel are not available even to fill the positions allowed by the budgets; waiting lists are horrendous. There is not much prospect of change.

Nevertheless, this huge process will change the climate of social work and its future. Physical planners are talking about social planning. They may hate social work—or, rather, despise it—they certainly do not understand it. But they know they have to have more of it. Their concentration at this time is on the human problem, no matter how badly they handle it.

There is benefit to the profession in aligning with it. There will be infinite benefit to the program, if it does so.

VALUES, ETHICS, AND FAMILY LIFE

by Joseph P. Fitzpatrick, S.J.

THE PRESUMPTION IS that America's children are suffering because of the widespread weakness and disintegration of family life. This weakness is due either to the fact that many parents do not have the necessary values to support strong family life, or, when they do have the necessary values themselves, the social environment makes it impossible for them to express these values in their family life.

In the United States, this problem develops in some instances from moral failure on the part of parents or other members of the community; in others, from the wide diversity of beliefs and values which are seriously held by responsible citizens; or, even where there is widespread agreement about particular values there is nevertheless no agreement as to whether they should be supported by law or by organized action of citizens, or left to the responsibility of each individual. This is the context of the problem.

What moral values are necessary for strong family life in the United States? In a pluralistic society, how can people be brought to a common agreement on these values? In the presence of diversity, how can we create a social environment which will support the commonly accepted values?

In order to approach this discussion in orderly fashion,

we must first clarify what we mean by "values"; then explain how values become related to social behavior and social structure; review the problem of values as it appears in American life; and examine some possibilities of improvement.

Very simply, a value is something I want or I do not want. I want an education; I want good health; I want political freedom; I want the freedom to worship God according to my conscience. These are values. I can speak of values in many different contexts: I can speak of the market value of a share of stock; the value of a detergent in washing clothes; the value of one type of reading instruction over another. We are concerned with moral values. A moral value is the definition of anything in relation to man's perfection and fulfillment as man, and to his ultimate destiny or purpose. What should a man want in order to fulfill himself as a man? This is consequent to answering the questions, What is man? For what is he destined? What is his fulfillment and perfection?

This is not directly a matter of how to clothe him or house him; how to keep him well or cure him when he is ill; how to train him as a youth or care for him in old age. These are technical matters which are closely related to moral values but which are not moral values in themselves. Even freedom itself is not a moral value. It is a situation in which man can pursue his moral values. Moral values, rather, touch on those intimate qualities of the human person which we call "virtues": the desire to know and to inquire; altruism in the service of others; devotion of husband to wife or wife to husband; respect of elders by children; integrity, courage, honesty; willingness to suffer for a cause, a moral purpose, a religious faith. These are the values that touch man in himself. They reflect, not what a man does or how he does it, but what he is. They relate, not to how he makes his living, but to what he does with his living after it is made.

There are three components in moral values. There is an element of faith, either religious faith that God has revealed what He wants me to do, or a humanistic faith that altruism and self-sacrifice, for instance, are noble human qualities. I emphasize this element of faith because it is obvious that the ultimate commitments of human life cannot be based on scientific evidence. Secondly, there is an element of human reason, the conviction of men that they can define the nature of man and the qualities which are necessary for his perfection. Finally, there is the wide range of social custom. These elements will come into our discussion later on. They have a great deal to do with the intensity with which people cling to particular values.

The real problem with moral values is not in defining what they are, but in defining more specifically how they are to be related to social behavior. There are two levels on which this takes place. In the first place, we have to define how the general moral values are to express themselves in specific forms of social behavior. Granted that marriage and family life are recognized as great moral values for the fulfillment of men and women, does the achievement of this moral value require monogamy, or does it permit polygamy? Does it require fidelity between husband and wife, or does it permit adultery? Does it restrict sexual relations to husband and wife, or permit it to the unmarried? Does it require permanence of the marriage bond, or does it permit divorce?

It is on this level that the serious problems begin to appear. There is probably a widespread acceptance of general moral values of integrity, devotion, unselfishness. It is in spelling these out in what we call the "moral code" or "moral principle" that the differences begin to appear. And these differences, which touch the heart of family life at every level, are held with deep conviction and proposed by serious citizens.

A further difficulty arises on the second level on which these values express themselves. For, even when there is agreement on a moral code, there will be cultural differences about its expression in a particular society. For instance, there is general agreement that husbands should respect their wives; wives should respect their husbands; and children should respect their parents. But respect will be defined differently in different cultures; even among different groups of the same culture. If a Mexican wife behaved toward her husband in the way a devoted middle-class American wife behaves toward hers, the Mexican husband would accuse her of serious disrespect. On the other hand, when a middle-class American wife sees what is considered "respectful" behavior on the part of a Mexican wife, she judges it to be insufferable subordination. In most immigrant families, a very strong exercise of authority was expected of the father; third-generation wives and children of the same immigrant group probably would not put up with that exercise of authority today. Many of the Latin people who come to the United States have a practice of careful chaperonage of the unmarried girl; this custom is ridiculed by American teen-agers even from the best of families.

It is important to note that this does not eliminate or even weaken the general moral principle. It simply means that certain forms of behavior become defined as respectful in our society, and others are defined as disrespectful. These definitions differ from one society to another; from one ethnic group to another; from one social class to another. The parents of American children do not want their children to be respectful to them in the way that Latin children are respectful to their parents. They want them to be respectful, as they would say, in an American way.

Nor are American parents less mindful of the chastity of their daughters than Latin parents are. They are convinced, however, that the American girl must be brought up to rely on herself. Both groups agree on the importance of the moral value of chastity. They differ about the ways by which the value must be protected.

In view of this, the serious problem concerning moral values is to determine when a form of behavior is a new manifestation of the same value; and when a form of behavior is the destruction of a value. This requires clear insight and good judgment.

This problem of the relationship of moral values to cultural definitions, in itself difficult enough, has been further complicated in the United States by two things: the meeting of large numbers of people from different cultural backgrounds; and the rapidity of social and cultural change in our society. In the first place, the experience of the uprooting weakened in the immigrant groups that spontaneous acceptance of common moral principles, the cultural definitions of these principles. What had been taken for granted as right for centuries, and what had been supported by a common culture, was now challenged by contact with other immigrant groups who defined their values in a different way, and by the dominant American culture which attracted the immigrant child away from the long-established norms of his ancestors. This need to adjust rapidly to a new set of cultural definitions of moral norms could not help but unsettle that firm, unquestioning adherence to patterns of behavior which made the paths of life so clear and well-trodden.

Together with the uprooting and the contact with people of other cultures, rapid social change has further complicated the cultural definition of moral values. In a century we changed from a rural to an urban people; technology created new patterns of relationships which we had not anticipated; the development of education and communication made new and challenging ideas the daily experience of millions.

In the presence of this kind of change, Americans have faced the problem of defining what the general moral values were to mean when they were expressed in American culture.

It is this lack of agreement on moral principles and on the cultural definition of the moral principles which makes the social support of moral values so difficult a problem. No moral value will be effective in a society unless it is strongly supported by the community, that is, until it has become a pattern of expected behavior, or, as a sociologist would say, unless it is institutionalized. It is true that a person can live according to values which run counter to the pattern of expected behavior in a society. But this requires extraordinary moral strength. And this extraordinary person's moral behavior will not begin to influence society until it has become widely accepted and supported.

This social support is given in two ways. Generally it is informal and expresses itself in the form of praise or reward to those who respect the moral values; criticism, ridicule, and indignation against those who do not respect the moral values. This is the social climate, as it were; the environment which makes a person sense what is expected of him in this society and what is not. The freedom given to American teen-agers in their courtship; the resistance of American families to interference from the in-laws; the ordinary expectation that the father will be the main support of the family; the expectation that families will seek to better themselves in American society—these and a hundred other big and little things are enforced by social pressure, informally exercised through praise or blame, through reward or ridicule.

In matters judged for one reason or another to be more serious, formal control is exercised through law. The law forbids polygamy; the law compels the father to support the child he has begotten; the law enforces the education of children; the law forbids divorce except under specific circumstances. One of the most difficult problems of political and social life is the decision when to support a moral value by positive law and when not to. If the informal social support for a moral value is strong enough, no law is needed; if the informal social support is very weak, no law will be effective. What political scientists call "consensus" must be present to a considerable degree to enable a law to be effective. The citizens of a community certainly have every right to seek the protection of law for the moral values they cherish. And when law is the reinforcement of strong consensus, it will be effective. This is not a question of "might makes right"; the right can be surprisingly helpless many times. It simply means that the enforcement of the right by law will be effective only under particular circumstances.

This has been a necessary preliminary to the real point of our discussion, the problem of moral values in the American family.

The signs of disorganization in the American family are easily recognized. Divorce, desertion, and abandonment are the dramatic evidences of failure; unhappiness and discontent in families which do not break up are less evident signs of the failure of the family to provide the enrichment it should. In many cases, mental illness, delinquent behavior, and alcoholism are the consequences of family weakness.

Family life, as all social life, is fundamentally the expression of values. And failure in family life is related to a failure of moral values on one of the levels I have already outlined. Let us look at some of these levels.

In the first place, let us look at the effect of some of the commonly accepted values of American family life. The central value of American culture is the fulfillment of the individual; ideally, it aims to provide the individual with every possible opportunity to develop himself and to reach that level of society to which his ability and effort entitle him. This is an extraordinary value, and I do not wish to appear to belittle it in any of my remarks. But as a result of this, our society has ceased to be familistic; it is predominantly individualistic. In other words, marriage and the family become interpreted in terms of personal fulfillment and happiness; not in terms of family strength. The success of the family is judged by norms of the personal satisfaction of each of its members. If the personal satisfaction is not achieved, there is strong encouragement to the couple to terminate the marriage. This is quite different from the strong family systems in other cultures, and even from the strong family systems of our immigrant ancestors who judged the family much more in terms of family strength than in terms of personal satisfaction. Marriage, in these systems, is considered much more a union of families than a union of two individuals. The central value of our culture, therefore, although it provides for a level of individual achievement never possible before, nevertheless pays a heavy price in family weakness for this individual fulfillment.

Secondly, another central value commonly accepted in our culture is the value of the social and economic advancement of the family. The central concern of most traditional families was economic survival. The central concern of most American families is social status, namely, the enjoyment of a level of living which is generally implied in the common phrase, "the American way of life." American parents wish to give their children the benefits of an American standard of living, and this requires an economic effort which is extraordinary. It frequently means two jobs for the husband; sometimes, employment for the wife. Again, I do not wish to belittle a value which has brought remarkable social and economic benefits to American families. But it demands a heavy price in family strain. For the economic activity which is pursued to advance the family creates a situation in which the family becomes subordinate to the economic activity. Decisions are made, not in terms of the human benefits of members of the family, but in terms of the economic advantages to be derived or, more commonly, in terms of the need to avoid economic losses which would drop the status of the family to a lower level. There is no need to document the anxiety and strain which are the classic difficulties of middle-class American life, and which result not from a confusion of values, but from commonly accepted values which are thoroughly institutionalized in American life.

These extraordinary efforts to achieve the values of American society would not be so risky if the rest of the value system were stable and clear. But, as I have indicated, in the area of more specific moral values, disagreement and controversy are widespread. We shall speak later about the social support of family values; but there is no agreement about what value to support. The anthropologists have pointed out the more serious consequences of this in the strange inconsistencies of our American culture. We have created a structure of family life which places a heavy burden of responsibility on the married couple; yet we permit and encourage a pattern of social relations which brings many young people into marriage before they are prepared for such responsibility. There is at least a strong theoretical condemnation of premarital sexual relations; yet the culture surrounds young people with an environment which is sexually stimulating while it punishes severely the unmarried girl who yields to the stimulus and becomes pregnant. The culture places a high premium on successful marriage, but emphasizes personal satisfaction to a point where it is a threat to the success of marriage. The culture encourages young people to leave their families of origin and set up a separate home of their own, but has thus far failed to settle the problem of the isolation of the aged. As a result, uncertainty is a common experience of married couples. They no longer have the clear, consistent guides to family living. Weakness can quickly deteriorate into disorganization.

Finally, there is the difficult problem of cultural change for the newcomers who face the process of integration into American life. There are impressive strengths as well as obvious weaknesses in the families of all these newcomers. But in the life from which they come, family played the central role. Whether they are the strong extended families or families which we consider problem families, of a mother and children without a husband, or a family with children of a number of different men, they come from cultures where a sense of family was a source of considerable strength, and where brothers, sisters, uncles, or grandparents were the great resource in the midst of all difficulties. The culture, in other words, created a situation in which these difficulties were not "social problems," in the sense in which they become problems in our large cities. But in the process of assimilation, the old patterns of social control are pulled apart; and the family loyalties tend to weaken.

When the newcomers start families without civil or religious marriage, I wonder what kind of an impression they get from our great effort to get them married. If this is simply a process of having them go through the routine of marriage in order to enjoy the legal benefits of marriage in the United States, I cannot see that they would be impressed by any moral values in their family life. In their old way of life, there was a clear recognition of things like devotion, loyalty, being good to one another. But the danger is great of their looking on marriage as a routine, especially when they know they can get out of it if it does not work. This hardly cultivates in them a deep sense of the moral values of marriage and family.

What kind of an approach can be taken to improve the situation?

It seems to me that we have to accept the individualistic emphasis of American family life. Within the framework of our kind of social and technological organization, I do not see how this can be avoided. Therefore, family strength will have to become more and more a personal responsibility rather than something that rests on the social organization, and American married couples will have to be prepared for the kind of dedication and determination which will be necessary for them to maintain this family stability. This means that communication of values will have to take place in a highly conscious and reflective way and a more than ordinary effort will have to be made through education and influence to bring American couples to realize the relationship of moral values to their family life. The achievement of family strength and stability through personal responsibility involves a great risk; but the possibilities of personal development and spiritual maturity are great also.

Secondly, values are rooted in faith; either in religious faith, by which I believe that God has taught me what to do; or in a humanistic faith, by which I rely on the spirit of man. Values are a commitment to some ultimate meaning in my life, and they cannot be established by empirical inquiry. It is in this sense that, in all social science literature, values are called a "nonrational" element. In all the societies of the past, faith has been the fundamental element in securing family values. Basically, in facing a crisis of family, we are facing a crisis of belief, of faith, of religion. I make this as a sociological judgment, not a theological one. What do men believe in? What is the ultimate meaning of marriage and family life? It seems to me that, in the sophisticated middle-class urban family, as well as in the Negro who has just arrived from Mississippi, or the newcomer from San Juan or Mexico City, there is a depth of religious faith which we often underestimate. This could be cultivated, brought more clearly to consciousness, made a reflective acceptance instead of a tradition that is taken for granted. This faith, related to family values, could be the strong underpinning of stable family living. I am not suggesting that religious faith is purely a social function. I am suggesting that we recognize the fundamental role that is played by man's commitment to an ultimate meaning in his life, and that we build our education for marriage on that fundamental commitment.

I am not very enthusiastic about the possibility that legal measures can contribute a great deal to the strengthening of family life. I think the great advances toward strong family life will have to come through education, social influence, public opinion, and the deepening of religious faith. I am impressed by the increasing agreement among social workers, social scientists and psychologists about the fundamental factors in healthy family living. Out of this will come a clearer understanding of man and his place in society, and an emphasis on the values necessary for strong family life.

THE CASE FOR DAY CARE

PANEL CHAIRMAN MRS. ELINOR GUGGENHEIMER: We shall call on key witnesses from various fields whose agencies deal with different kinds of problems in our society and ask each to testify briefly about day care in relation to his particular area of concern.

JOSEPH H. REID: I was asked to testify for children in a city. Literally thousands of people every month pick themselves up from the rural areas and migrate to the large cities. Almost one third of all American families move every year in the United States, and often these moves mean a complete change in environment. Although day care is perhaps the oldest form of child welfare service in our country—at least to the extent that children were and are left during the day with a nurse, a neighbor, a relative, or a friend—it is a service that a family loses when it moves away from its established neighborhood and comes to a large city. No matter what the cause of the need, whether the mother is working or the family is in difficulty, day care is extremely difficult for a newcomer to find in our large cities. Families in trouble have access to a variety of child welfare services, such as full-time foster care treatment for an emotionally disturbed child, family counseling, but rarely can day care service be found. I suspect a great part of the lack is the fault of professionals in the field. Day care does not evoke the interest aroused by treatment of disturbed children, nor does it offer the glamour of family counseling or the drama of psychiatric service. Families seeking it do not find much interest in, or knowledge of, day care on the part of the experts and agencies to which they turn.

Yet, like any other public service, day care should be available in any city—widely available and without the necessity of going through a diagnostic service. It should be acknowledged as a component of our modern technological civilization. Moreover, because of the enormous changes that are taking place in scientific technology, it follows that there is a demand for people to change their pattern of life and culture in order to meet those changes. Out of these changes has come the as yet unmet need for good day care service for children.

In our large cities we find in basement windows dozens of signs announcing that someone who takes care of children has a "vacancy." Newspapers advertise child care. This type of care is a form of baby-sitting service where youngsters can stay while their mothers are away from home. But the ways in which the children's emotional and educational needs are met leaves very, very much to be desired. We are only beginning to license these facilities and we are only beginning to be aware of these needs.

In many of our large cities day care is almost an unknown service. Thus, thousands of children go, unnecessarily, into other, more expensive forms of care which do not meet their needs—a consequence of our failure to recognize the importance of such facilities.

CLARK W. BLACKBURN: The Family Service Association of America (FSAA) is interested in strengthening family life. We do a great deal of counseling with families, and most of this is done after something has happened. I want to stress particularly that, as time goes on, the FSAA will try to take more and more leadership to see if we cannot do more preventive work. The profession talks a great deal about prevention, but we must see if we cannot do more— much as Public Health has done—to get a preventive social welfare policy. One hears of primary prevention, secondary prevention, and so on, but it is important to keep in mind that if we are going to prevent trouble we must do something to help families *now* so that the adults of the future will make better parents.

Here are a few facts about broken families where there are children under six years of age. According to the most recent United States census, the number of children who are living with one parent only totals 1,897,000. Of this group only a little over 6 percent are with the father, so the great bulk of these children are with the mother. Now, we can imagine what happens in these families where there is just the one parent. We know that there are serious deficiencies. One of the first questions is: How will a family be supported if there is no male breadwinner?

We have our insurances, our public assistance plans, and certainly we are concerned with the problem faced by the mothers who are needed at home with children aged, say, from three to six. Some type of care is necessary, but we should establish what kind of care is needed.

Our training in social welfare taught us that a child needs two parents. If a mother who is alone puts a child in a day care center, and this is run by women, where does the child get an image of what a male is like? I think that should be thought about, and somehow we should get more men interested in day care as a way of giving children a more rounded program. Foster family day care would solve this problem to some extent.

I am not saying that day care is the one method for handling all the children of these broken homes, but it is one important method, and I am emphatic in saying that I think we should have many more day care centers than we do have.

MRS. LAURA LEE SPENCER: On behalf of the Women's Bureau I am happy to present the case for day care in the interests of the working mother. In considering the need for day care for children of working mothers, we have to answer the question: Why is the working mother a part of our social system or a part of our community?

We see more women working everywhere. There are more women in political life. There are more women doctors. There are more women lawyers. There are women porters and women who drive taxicabs. In spite of this, there are still undercurrents that woman's place is in the home, and statements that day care facilities will just send more women into the labor market to take jobs away from the men.

I was interested to see in the *Wall Street Journal* in April an article discussing the job market situation and the increased participation of women in the labor force. The author commented that women are able to leave the home and join the working force because of frozen foods, ready-prepared foods, instant foods, automatic dishwashers, laundromats, diaper services, and day nurseries.

Well, ladies and gentlemen of the jury, if you are going to decide this case you should look at the evidence and look at the figures and look at the reasons why there are women working in order to understand why we need day care for the children of working mothers.

In 1960 there were over 64,000,000 women in the United States and more than 22,000,000 women working. There were over 12,000,000 working women in families that had husbands present. There were about 10,000,000 working women who were unmarried: they were divorced; they were widowed; and they were single women living alone.

Now, these 10,000,000 women were supporting themselves. It was necessary that they work. In the same year, 1960, of the 14,000,000 women in the United States who had children under six years of age, 3,000,000 were employed. Of this number there were over one million women without partners who had children under six. This makes a large number of women who had to plan for the care of their children while employed.

There have been many studies which have indicated that there is a direct correlation between the number of working married women and the income level of their husbands. For example, 27 percent of children under eighteen are in families where the father earns less than $2,000 a year, and these are families in which the mother is also employed.

Recently, the Bureau of Labor Statistics analyzed some previously unpublished figures which offer a somewhat better guide for determining the need for married women to work. They analyzed the figures which they had collected for their consumer budget survey in 1950. At that time a city worker's family budget was set up, correlated with family income, which would provide for minimum family nurture. It was found that in 42 percent of families where women were working, the income was below that required by the city worker's family budget.

Now, what happens to all these children of working mothers and to the working mother herself? A survey which was made by the census for the Children's Bureau indicated that of a total of 5,000,000 children, there were approximately 400,000 who had to look after themselves and there were over 647,000 children who were classified as having other kinds of care. These two groups are the children who need some sort of planned, systematic care because, in addition to being latchkey children, they may be the children who go to playgrounds of their own volition or just visit neighbors.

In the Women's Bureau we are interested in the advancement of the working woman and we are interested in services for the working woman, which includes day care.

CYRUS H. KARRAKER: I am a highly prejudiced witness because I have been a crusader in behalf of the migrant laborers and their children for the past ten years.

The fact is that our government a few years ago was spending $650 million on migratory birds and nothing on migrant children.

Of the estimated 1,500,000 migrants in America, about 50,000 are children of preschool age.

These children remind one of the factory children of a hundred years ago who lived in the slums and worked in the sweatshops. The migrant children live on farms; as young as five years of age they work in the fields. They are neglected, except for the very few who are under supervised care. The majority are neglected in education, health, love and care, and happiness. They are deprived of the rights and the fun and the enjoyment which all children should have.

My state is Pennsylvania. It was Pennsylvania that first,

in 1954, set up a day care center for the children of migrant families. Child welfare service is provided for all other dependent children. There is no residence requirement for them, so why should there be for these children? Now there are eight centers in the state, operated with Federal funds.

This is my point: Money is available through child welfare services, and more is in prospect than ever before. Money is therefore available for migrant children, and the best place to use it is in day care; but the states are not using this money. There should be no isolation of day care from the camp and from the community. As I see it, day care centers of the Pennsylvania type are badly needed today, and the Federal government must be prevailed upon to take the leadership in providing funds to set up these centers.

SISTER SERENA: I am pleased to speak on behalf of emotionally disturbed and mentally retarded children. Anyone who works with these children knows the benefits that can be attained and is quite aware that their need is an obvious one. These two groups of children represent two of our major health problems. On any given day there are almost 20,000 children in the psychiatric hospitals of this country. More than half a million children are mentally ill, and the national organization for mentally ill children says that only one percent of these children are receiving adequate treatment.

Certainly it is our responsibility to help stem the tide of mental illness, and it has to be done through prevention. We know that there is a direct relationship between mental illness and gross social family pathology. We are aware of this and aware of its impact.

Nationally, the number of these children is increasing,

and, by sheer weight of the growth of our population, we are going to have more disturbed children. Also, progress in medicine is saving more children. The premature babies are being spared. Medical people are aware of cortical disability in many of these infants, and we are faced with new numbers of "brain-injured" children. These children are a problem to our schools, a problem to parents, and they are really the victims of medical progress. But they are with us, and we have to do something about it.

Regardless of ideology or causation, we know that in emotionally disturbed children the disequilibrium manifests itself in some maladaptive behavior. In the early decades of our century we had the syndrome of hysteria.

What do we have now? A large percentage of the emotionally disturbed are affected by character disorders. These children may be chronic truants; hyperactive, aggressive children; the manipulative, affectionless children who disrupt foster home after foster home; primitive children who are unable to socialize. We have the brain-injured children and the psychiatric population. In any event, these children with varying degrees of disturbances do need care. We know there must be a broad spectrum of services. There will always be room for more family counseling and child guidance agencies to work with these children at the point where the disturbance manifests itself.

The severely affected children will need the closed halls of state hospitals. Unfortunately, the number of residential treatment centers is far from adequate. Moreover, residential treatment centers are very expensive; each has, on the average, from twenty to thirty-five beds. In a society that needs so much more, that is not going to be the answer. And so we are still groping.

I am convinced that if we could operate day treatment centers for disturbed children much as we operate our residential treatment centers, we could help these youngsters. A multidisciplined staff working as a team could set up the regimen with an understanding of the various needs of the children and plan their program individual by individual, giving each child the structure and the strength that come from nurturing by adults with whom they can form some type of satisfactory relationship. We could see the parents more frequently, for their cooperation would be needed. We could keep the parents informed and try to change their tactics. However, we know that we have not been able to do all this because we do not have the financial resources. We do not have the staff. But somehow I think we can train staff, and we could get staff if we had the money.

The benefits of day care for emotionally disturbed children are many. We could accept the child before his problem became fixed and intensified; there would be the favorable position of working more closely with the family and more intimately with the parents; usually parents are less resistive to placing a child in treatment if they do not have to surrender him for twenty-four hours at a time; the day treatment center should be less costly than large centers and could be handled with facility.

We have, too, increased numbers of retarded children by virtue of the population growth. We have 5,500,000 retardates now, and it is expected that by 1970 there will be an additional million. Unfortunately, very little was done for such people, except in isolated instances in the nineteenth century, until the 1950s when a group of parents banded together and founded the National Association for

Retarded Children, which has been responsible for tremendous progress on all fronts. They are forging ahead, and now they have professional people with them who are backing them up.

We see the need for a broad spectrum of service, a comprehensive program of coordinated services with a multi-discipline and multi-agency approach, a coordinated community attack city by city, state by state. These services would provide diagnosis, treatment, and family counseling. The children would go from home training through the nursery schools, the day centers, the classes for both the educable and trainable child of school age in our schools, and workshops and occupational day centers. It is obvious that if these parents are to obtain any kind of encouragement and support; if they are to be helped to see what the problem of their handicapped child is; and if they can be helped to see how they can adapt their knowledge to their own method of handling the child intelligently, this is their right.

We have an obligation to give them this kind of service. While the schools handle 80 percent of the educable retarded children of school age, there are trainable children who are simply too retarded to fit into the public school program and children who are too young. Research has shown us that these children can be tremendously benefited if they receive attention early enough. These are the ones who are young enough for day care. We must offer some ray of relief to parents of handicapped children and to the normal child in the family as well. If they do not get some relief, the normal child is then deprived, while the fact that someone is working with them tends to relieve the parents' emotional stress and disturbance. They have the opportunity to take part in all types of educational and recreational programs conducted by day centers. Thus, there is no need to institutionalize a child if he can get help on the home front, and the parents will not have to resort to the use of state facilities.

It is probable that no other single event affects so profoundly the equilibrium of family life as the birth of a severely retarded child or a severely handicapped child. Any effort on the part of society to lessen the trauma is well worth the time, money, and effort expended. Day care, it seems, offers these positive benefits.

MRS. GRACE HOLMES BARBEY: The witnesses thus far have considered the problem of children from broken homes, children of working mothers, children in migratory areas and of the migrants themselves, the handicapped, and the emotionally disturbed. My concern is with the children of the world and involves all of these.

The variety of day care services goes from one extreme to the other. One can see fine day care centers in the most squalid areas in the world. On the water's edge at Lagos in Nigeria a group of women developed an excellent center because of the problem of the working mothers and the unsupervised youngsters. Egypt has a fine program sponsored by the Cairo Women's Club in rural as well as urban areas. Japan has had for some time a broad program of services.

The United Kingdom has a different type of operation. The Ministry of Education operates one day care program, and the center is usually open from nine to four. In Austria, factories have amazing day care centers. At the end of the Second World War there was a day care center in the French Zone of Vienna with youngsters from, perhaps, five to six months old on up to a twelve-year-old boy who had once won a poster contest for the United Nations Children's Fund (UNICEF).

Sweden and Switzerland have been outstanding. Australia, New Zealand, and Canada have day camps located in mother-child welfare clinics.

One of the most developed day care programs is in the USSR. Russia is different from our own country—everyone must work and work very hard, yet the great majority of Soviet children continue to be reared in their own homes by their own families. From 12 percent to 20 percent are under the attention of a day care center. The rest of them are watched over either by a grandmother or by a neighbor. Of course, the aim is to have most of the children under some kind of care during the day. Primarily, the Russians believe that the goal is to have the best care they can possibly have for their children because that will be to the benefit of the state. This is true in Poland, Romania, and Czechoslovakia in varying degrees. UNICEF, along with the Bureau of Social Affairs and all the other United Nations groups, has just begun to get into this type of program.

MRS. MARIANA JESSEN: As one of the child welfare services in our highly mobile society, the day care program deals with children in their own homes and communities, while the children for whom other child welfare services are designed have been removed from such communities. Children do not easily or automatically conform to the standards set by an institution for full-time care. The children are placed in such an institution as a result of a long series of community failures to meet the families' needs and prevent the breakdown. If we can begin more effectively and more frequently to avoid the wrenching full-time separation from the family, avoid that final rejection; if we can begin to see the problem at the beginning, then we can regard the institution or the foster home and adoption agency as the final, carefully thought-through solution rather than as an unfortunate expedient. Day care can then serve as both a preventive and a curative child welfare service. Preventive services are very expensive but not nearly so expensive as those costly social ills which result from that lack of quality in care which is so essential in the very young years.

Young children come from young families, and young families in trouble may often be helped before the breakdown occurs. The tensions caused by overcrowded housing, illness, poverty, or related causes can be relieved for the family and the child by a good day care service.

We too often think of day care as a service for children of working mothers. Those of us who have been connected with the program, however, know that the staff of a good center carefully studies the needs of parents and child and recommends day care only when this seems to be the best possible plan. Sometimes a counselor can persuade a mother not to seek employment if the best interests of a child require her presence at home. There are also circumstances which indicate that for the welfare of the mother, or in order to break away from a two-or-three-generation pattern of dependency, it may be advisable to help her to find employment. It would be ideal if the determination whether a mother should work or stay at home could always be made with the help of skilled counseling. We know that only under extenuating circumstances would we in the National Committee for the Day Care of Children recommend employment; otherwise, we urge as many mothers as possible not to leave young children during the day. The program is not designed solely to serve working mothers. We have an increasing number of children from families where the mother is ill or disturbed, or where social factors or the emotional need of the child play a part. Nevertheless, a large number of children whose families cannot provide good day care come from situations where the mothers must work. Economic need is a potent factor in the decision of the mother, and certainly we ought to review the effectiveness of the present Aid to Dependent Children scale of payment since ADC has proved of such little persuasion in holding mothers in the home.

Statistics reveal that whether there is adequate day care or not, growing numbers of mothers are entering the labor force. There are licensed day care facilities for 185,000 children in our country. There are at least 400,000 children for whom no arrangements whatsoever are made for care during the day. Where are they? The most acute neglect suffered by the children of two groups of working mothers remains a national disgrace. The slum children and those who live in the migrant farm camps may be reached and helped only if we set up day care centers properly financed and licensed by the states.

For another group of children—the deaf, the blind, the cardiac cases, the crippled, the cerebral palsied, the retarded, the emotionally disturbed—we have begun to discover that day care can open a door into the normal community. If he does not have the service in his early years, it may become impossible to improve the condition of a potentially adjustable child. We may leave some of these children permanently imprisoned by their own handicaps.

They should be provided with day care centers, whether specialized or not, where they can be absorbed, much like less handicapped children, into helpful programs as well as given an opportunity to live in a supervised situation and to develop a good relationship with an adult. In turn, this can lead to a better relationship between a child and his mother, who may not previously have emotionally comprehended the problem.

These are the factors which make day care imperative. These families and these children need help. We have lagged dangerously behind other countries in this type of program. In almost every country in the world the government has assumed responsibility for at least part of the operating costs of day care. In Norway, Finland, France, the United Kingdom, Yugoslavia and all the Communist countries, and most of the countries in Africa, day care is a prime concern of the government. In the United States there are no Federal funds for day care except for a very limited type of service. We spend millions in an effort to stay strong with weapons of defense. Our children are certainly as important as the weapons; and they are the only true answer to survival, not only of our country but of the world.

Therefore, Your Honor, ladies and gentlemen of the jury, I plead for aid for the children and for their families, for those in the urban areas and in migrant farm camps, and for the handicapped, so that we can continue to show other countries that the basic ingredient of a democracy continues to be concern for the individual. I believe that this country must develop day care centers for its children with the best possible trained supervision, with safe and attractive facilities, carefully planned and properly financed, so that at all times for every child in every community we shall be able to answer the question: "Where is the child?" Your Honor, the case for day care rests.

GROUP EDUCATION FOR CHILD REARING

by Aline B. Auerbach

A PARADOX AND A CHALLENGE face all who are concerned with the mental health of children and families. On the one hand, new knowledge "from behavioral and social sciences and from empirical and research sources" supports the belief that "a strong family is the keystone of a free and healthy society" in which, it is to be hoped, all the family members may have the opportunity for optimal functioning in their given situations. Yet at the same time, there are "compelling forces in the modern world" that threaten "the stability and strength of family life." Each of us might describe these forces in his own way. But might we perhaps agree that the geographic and social mobility so characteristic of our times tends to cut off many young families from their traditional moorings and leaves them vulnerable to a wide range of conflicting pressures and uncertainties? Their constantly increasing exposure to new ideas through contact with new people and the stimulation of the mass media opens the way for enriched experiences. It also challenges them to evaluate their goals for themselves as individuals and for the family as a whole. They need to think through how they may choose to achieve these goals: either trying new ways, if the old ones have not been adequate or satisfying; or adhering to the old ones, if on thoughtful consideration these seem to be sound.

Can education for child rearing be of help to families in this general situation? What are the contributions and limitations of group educational approaches in building family strengths?

Obviously, we are not talking here about those educational experiences which are the usual responsibility of the teaching profession and which are conducted under formal educational auspices. Rather we are referring to broadly educational services and programs that deal with family life and child rearing, in which social workers are becoming increasingly involved, either conducting them under the auspices of their agencies or acting on loan, as it were, to groups meeting under a variety of other auspices. These activities are not confined to any one discipline. Psychologists, public health and hospital nurses, physicians, and home economists are asked to conduct these activities, as are many persons from educational systems at all levels. The difference is perhaps primarily in the settings—which may be of many kinds—and, more essentially, in the nature, focus, and methodology of the programs.

Chiefly, group education for family living at its most thoughtful, recognizes that learning is more than an abstract intellectual process. It provides for the acquisition of new information, of course, as a means of enlarging the perspective and broadening the point of view of those who attend—information about phases of psychological growth and development, the inner meaning of behavior, the complexities of family interplay, and so on. This information is obtained from the members in the discussion, brought into balance, if necessary, or underscored by the leader, who also contributes further information. But group education also includes as an important part of its content the examination of the members' feelings and attitudes. This is especially significant since the group educational experience is focused on the members' daily lives and their interpersonal relations. Finally, it takes into account the fact that learning takes place in the group and, to the extent that it is possible within the plan and structure of the particular program, it makes conscious use of the group as an additional tool to enhance and enrich individual learning. (Conventional teaching in academic settings is being carried on within these concepts, too, of course, to an ever increasing degree—selectively, according to the implications of the subject areas that are being taught.) These distinctions may seem almost too obvious to warrant defining, but they need to be made explicit, as a base of reference.

Even this brief summarization is difficult because group educational opportunities are of many kinds and use many different techniques. Even the prevalent single meeting on child rearing has almost as many forms as the individuals who take on the job of conducting them. And even in single meetings, speakers or leaders, depending on their concept of their roles, consciously or intuitively adapt their approach to the size of the audience and even to such seemingly unimportant circumstances as the arrangement of the chairs. Meetings that deal with children and family living take the form of lectures, film showings, plays, group discussions, singly or in series. These programs, in turn, are merely a part of a total spectrum of services to parents and families. At one end, one finds the information-giving approaches of the various mass media. Group educational activities fall somewhere in the middle, together with individual educational counseling in those situations which lend themselves to an individualized approach. Beyond the educational spectrum are services that offer intensive counseling or therapy on an individual or group basis. The mere listing of these services suggests the variety of motivations and needs that require a selective use of a wide range of services.[1]

It is important to define the purposes and goals of group educational services for family living even while we recognize their diversity. We must face as honestly as we can the extent to which they can be expected realistically to achieve these goals. All have a basic common purpose. Where they are offered to parents, they aim to help them become more familiar with basic concepts of child growth and development and of parent-child family interaction from a dynamic point of view; to recognize some of the crisis points at different stages of the normal family circle; to clarify the parents' own role, and those of their children, within the family and in the community; and to enlarge their understanding of the complexities of their everyday situations so that they will have a wider background against which to make choices.

Group educational services to young people—in high school or college; or later, before or after marriage—have similar goals, related, however, to the specific phase of the family life cycle in which they find themselves. It is difficult to prepare young people in advance for their specific emotional responses to their roles as marriage partners

[1] Aline B. Auerbach, *Trends and Techniques in Parent Education: a Critical Review* (New York: Child Study Association of America, 1961); Gertrude Goller, *When Parents Get Together* (New York: Child Study Association of America, 1955).

and parents. This is especially true since many of them are intensely involved in working out their current problems of identity and relationships. Out of these very struggles and concerns, however, they can gain self-knowledge and some understanding of the interplay of personalities in the family. They can also develop a general point of view about human relations which can stand them in good stead as they move into their new roles.

In the experience of the Child Study Association of America, the type of group education that comes closest to achieving these broad goals is the small continuous discussion group of approximately fifteen members which meets for a series of eight to twelve weekly sessions under skilled leadership. This approach has been used in a variety of programs under the Association's auspices for parents of children of different ages, for expectant parents (either for mothers alone or for couples), and for parents of handicapped children. Parent group education has also been the focus of training programs for group education leadership given by the Association to social workers, nurses, educators, and so on. The method has been defined and clarified by the Association's training staff, with the help of an advisory committee. A guest faculty, drawn from medicine (including psychiatry), psychology, education, cultural anthropology, and so forth, has contributed to the training programs, the details of which have been described in the Association's publications.[2] Parent groups held at the association and in many parts of the country in connection with the various training programs (whose leaders

[2] "A Program of Professional Training for Discussion Group Leadership in Mental Health Education for Family Living" (New York: Child Study Association of America, 1962).

have been closely supervised by the training staff) have presented a growing mass of experience for thoughtful study. They present convincing evidence that group education of this kind, sensitively carried out, is one important means of helping individuals to cope more effectively with the needs of their family members, even under difficult and trying circumstances.

In groups of this kind, many of the goals we have defined can be achieved, though in varying degrees, since the number of sessions is still small. Here, the discussion is based on the interests and concerns of the group members rather than on a topic-oriented curriculum or outline. Through the group interplay, the parents have an opportunity to bring out their own feelings and ideas, their hopes and disappointments, and to look at their children more objectively as they hear about other children in similar everyday situations.

They need to be helped also to look at themselves, as other group members are looking at themselves, to find out what they know—which is often more than they think— and what they need to know, thoughtfully to examine their own emotional responses and to check them against the realities, sometimes even coming to see from where these responses may have come.

Through the exchange of ideas and experiences, which are given life and individuality by the special coloration of the persons who voice them, each member moves to find his own place, to know where he stands. Slowly, as he agrees with some and differs with others, he begins to discover for himself what it is he wants to do in his situation. With the help of the leader, he also comes to learn how to evaluate an issue, to look at its many sides and see a little more

clearly its implications for all who are involved. This is a
kind of problem-solving, if you will, that can be used in
many different situations once it has become part of a
person. As Caplan has said,

There is a good deal of justification for thinking that the capacity
for reality-based problem-solving is an excellent measure of the
mental health of an individual or a group, and also for thinking that the way people handle any significant stress situation
in a crisis will have far-reaching effects on their future mental
health.[3]

Summarized excerpts from two group educational meetings will illustrate some of the many subtle ways in which
members gain further understanding of their situations
and of themselves.

From a group of parents of children of nursery school age:

In the sixth session of a group for parents of children from 3
to 5 years of age, meeting in a school setting, several mothers
and fathers shared their annoyance with the difficult behavior
of their first-born 5-year-olds who were bossy to their younger
siblings and gave them no peace. Other parents brought out a
variety of different kinds of behavior in their children of the
same age, so the group felt that the behavior could not be
accounted for either on the basis of the age or the sex of the
children or even of their ordinal position. They began to look
backward, and the three parents, around whose children the
discussion had started, found that they had been deeply concerned for their first children at the time the second ones had
been born, and, in varying degrees, had almost neglected the
new baby in order to concentrate on the first one "so that he
wouldn't feel too upset." Again, other members discussed the
different reactions and ideas they had had in similar situations.
Suddenly, the mother of one of the aggressive older children

[3] Gerald Caplan, M.D., *An Approach to Community Mental Health*
(New York: Grune and Stratton, 1961), p. 7.

burst out, "I've just discovered something most interesting." She added that Mr. D., whose child was also one of the troublesome youngsters and with whom she had been talking quietly on the side, was the first-born in his family, and she and her husband had also been the oldest in theirs. "I guess," she went on more slowly, "perhaps that is why we have all been so eager to spare our children the heartaches that come when there's a new baby in the family. Perhaps we all remembered our own feelings better than we knew!" The group was silent for a moment. Then there was a rush of corroboration—and of different viewpoints, epitomized by another mother who said quite poignantly that she hadn't had any trouble with her little girl when the second one came, but that perhaps she hadn't worried about the child's being jealous; she had been an only child herself, and could only feel happy that her daughter would have a sister or brother as a companion! For the better part of what was left of the meeting, the members discussed thoughtfully how their own experiences may have colored their feelings and their behavior toward their children.

From a group of parents of handicapped children:

This was the first meeting of quite a different group, a small one of mothers of young blind children, some of whom had multiple handicaps. About half way through the session, the mothers began to pour out how their husbands felt about their handicapped little ones and how their husbands' bitterness affected the relations between husband and wife. One mother said her husband blamed himself for having gotten her pregnant and therefore felt responsible for having created a handicapped child. Another said her husband blamed her for working until her baby was born prematurely; since she was a nurse, he said, she should have known better. The leader encouraged other group members to share some of their and their husbands' reactions to their first knowledge of their babies' conditions. The mothers soon shifted to their own feelings and voiced a wide range of responses, from being grateful that the baby had lived at all to some expression of their own guilt and disappointment. The leader attempted to get the group to explore the extent to which they or their husbands were, in fact, actually responsible for their children's disabilities. For a brief while, they talked about how little is known about the real causes of birth defects, but they did not stay with this topic very long. It seemed as if at this first session they needed to go back to the beginning, as if they had to reexperience their and their husbands' grief and mourning within the protection of the group; here other people had had similar situations, and it was all right for them to talk as they felt. The leader did not press the group to move on. She reported, however, that after they had described in great detail the full circumstances of their children's birth and first few days of life and had shared much of what they had thought and felt, some of the sadness and bitterness seemed to have moderated. Only then did they begin to talk about their children's current behavior and the concerns they had about them.

These fragments are small pieces of a process which takes place over a period of weeks. They are introduced here merely to suggest their implications for building family strengths through an educational approach in which the members examine facts and feelings, hopes and fears, the present in the light of the past and the implications for the future. In its philosophy, goals, and techniques, this is group education and not group therapy. Individuals come to the meetings for a common learning experience; they are not selected or referred because of pathology. Group education is of help to members who have problems or concerns, but the concerns are conscious, or close to consciousness, and are accessible for exploration. Group education cannot be expected to help those whose problems lie close to the core of a deep-rooted, emotional disturbance. Obviously, for such individuals some therapeutic help is indicated. Yet it has been found that many persons who have some degree of neurotic conflict can often gain from group education, developing ego strengths which enable them to function despite or around the areas of conflict. The goal is not to effect deep personality change; it is rather to increase the members' personal competence through a better understanding of themselves and their situations and to open up many alternatives from which they can choose ways to meet them. Often new understanding and new competence bring some shifts in attitudes; these, in turn, often bring about changes in the home climate and in the behavior of the family members as well.

It is this primary focus on more effective ego functioning that holds great promise for parents, helping them to meet present situations more effectively and to forestall future difficulties. Toward this end, parent group leadership draws heavily on both casework and social group work.[4] It adapts some of the basic concepts of both toward helping the group members with their concerns about their family and child-rearing problems, in terms of "where they are." This approach seems to be particularly effective in clarifying stress points in family life and enabling young people to understand and deal with the normal crises that come as they take on new roles in the family cycle, first as husband and wife and then as parents who must learn to cope with the needs of their children at different stages of growth.

Since in group education the skills of group discussion are directed to special areas of content, it has, of course, been used for group learning that has to do with many

[4] Mildred Rabinow and Oscar Rabinowitz, "The Use of Casework Concepts in Parent Group Education," in *Casework Papers, 1961* (New York: Family Service Association of America, 1961), pp. 131–42; Ada M. Daniels and Ernest Weinrich, "The Role of Social Group Work in Parent Group Education with Parents of Children with Disabilities: Fostering Rehabilitation Goals," paper presented at the National Conference on Social Welfare, 1962.

aspects of personal growth within the family. Many classes in family life education in the schools, again, follow the lines of more didactic teaching in connection with a syllabus or outline, but many are also using discussion methods around the students' current concerns about themselves and their intrafamilial and interpersonal relations. Groups of young people coming together in many settings for preparation for marriage, or to discuss aspects of marital adjustment are also using this approach. It seems to be particularly effective, as compared with the more usual curriculum-oriented approach, with expectant parents, both in mothers' and couples' classes. And parents of handicapped children and even parents of handicapped young adults are also taking advantage of this type of group educational experience. The possibilities are endless.

But how much of this can be accomplished in other types of programs—in shorter series of meetings, for example, or even in single sessions and in larger groups in which little use can be made of the interplay between the group members? Obviously, one has to shift one's goals, depending upon the duration of the experience and the extent to which it is based on the real needs of the participants and draws them into the program with a feeling of involvement. The answer seems to lie in the magic gift of the speaker or leader to sense, out of sympathy and wide experience, where people are confused, and to conceptualize, out of knowledge "in depth," interpretations about family behavior that open up for the audience a new integration of intellectual knowledge with the emotional side of human experience. Such a spark can touch off what is close to consciousness, leading a mother, a father, a young husband, a wife, to think about their reactions to these ideas, to sort out where they agree with them and where they do not, and to begin to work through some of their emotional responses as well. But in most cases this is hard to do alone, or even in pairs, without further stimulation and professional help. Single meetings or short series can also be effective within their natural limitations, opening the way for individual counseling or for more extended group experience, within either an educational or a therapeutic program, according to the individual's needs.

More positively, however, all group educational experiences can present a point of view which in itself is not to be minimized. This can be implied or made explicit in varying degrees. Within the philosophy of the Child Study Association, this point of view would include some of these basic concepts:

1. Each person needs to work out his own place and functioning in his family life in his own way, with his own measure of human frailty and his great human potential.

2. All people need to learn to get along with others, recognizing differences in innate endowment and temperament. Parents need to know and learn to gear in to the special natures and needs of their children, just as children need to learn to "mesh" in special ways with their parents and siblings.

3. The behavioral sciences are constantly broadening our knowledge of human behavior in ways that have implications for the everyday life of the family. New information about child growth and development and family interaction, for example, often gives meaning to what family members say they half-knew already, or adds interpretations into which bits of puzzling behavior fit like pieces of a jigsaw puzzle.

4. All behavior carries with it the potential for positive and negative feelings, as part of human experience. Individuals often need encouragement to face both aspects and put them in perspective.

5. The primary purpose of education is not reassurance, as is often stated, but honest recognition of anxiety when it exists and examination of the realities on which it is based.

6. While many of these concepts can be acquired individually through reading or in one-to-one social or professional relations, they are often gained more effectively in groups of peers, where the group process itself seems to facilitate an individual's development of his own distinctive point of view. (It must be repeated, however, that if a person has a deep emotional block, he may achieve some intellectual understanding of a situation or a relationship but may not be able to put this into practice, since he is not responding to it wholly.)

Group education for family living falls well within the province of social workers. In the Association's experience, they bring to this activity a rich background on which to build and the high degree of self-awareness which is so essential for group leadership. As yet, the curricula of schools of social work have not included training in educational group leadership in this field. Consequently, special projects have been set up, such as the Child Study Association's training programs and in-service opportunities for the staffs of individual agencies. There is, however, a growing interest in this approach as one means of promoting family health and strengths. As more programs for improved family living are developed under social agency auspices, we hope that there will be much experimentation to sharpen procedures in group educational methods and to explore whatever content is needed both by caseworkers and by group workers.[5] There is also the need for more sensitive evaluative research, since research to date has not been as useful as had been hoped.[6] There are, however, many new stirrings which indicate that research in the next few years will throw much light on the crisis points in family life and ways in which family members may be helped to meet them.[7]

In the meantime, we can only reaffirm our conviction, based on long experience and pooled professional judgment, that all family members have potential capacities and capabilities that are too often ignored. The task of developing these potentials challenges the helping professions to rethink the ways in which professional knowledge can best be made accessible and meaningful to wider segments of the population. In spreading our targets, however, we shall, I hope, continue to function within the democratic philosophy of education, which holds firmly to the belief that each person must use knowledge and understanding in his own way.

[5] Aline B. Auerbach and Gertrude Goller, "The Contribution of the Professionally Trained Leader of Parent Discussion Groups," *Marriage and Family Living*, XV (1953), 265–69; Aline B. Auerbach, "Family Life Education as a Service of the Casework Agency," *Jewish Social Service Quarterly*, XXXI (1955), 316–24.

[6] Orville G. Brim, Jr., *Education for Child Rearing* (New York: Russell Sage Foundation, 1959).

[7] Gerald Caplan, M.D., "An Approach to the Study of Family Mental Health," in Iago Galdston, M.D., ed., *The Family: a Focal Point in Health Education* (New York: International Universities Press, 1961), pp. 52–73; John C. Glidewell, ed., *Parental Attitudes and Child Behavior* (Springfield, Ill.: Charles C. Thomas, 1961).

RECREATION AND FAMILY NEEDS

by Ruth S. Tefferteller

I HAVE NEVER MET a family that takes pride in being weak, that boasts about its problems, that values disorganization or praises children who defy authority. On the contrary, there is, I believe, a basic longing in every family to live up to the expectations of society, to live according to the golden rule, to make a good impression on neighbors, teachers, social worker, minister—the neighborhood as a whole, in fact—and an equivalent longing for some recognition of their efforts to achieve this. It is imperative that we proceed on the assumption that this longing to be a good family is fundamental among the greatest majority and that along with this exists a craving for satisfactory fulfillment.

Organization of group work and recreation services in such a way as to provide opportunities for more family activities—giving families a chance to perform as families, to mingle with, and learn from, other families—should be one of the primary objectives of social work agencies. For it is well known to the profession that many families fall short of their fulfillment and increasingly need the chance to find their strengths, to exercise their family identity, and to feel their family vitality through special kinds of experiences.

The fields of group work and recreation, with their

special skills for developing programs and techniques which build group strength and solidarity, seem peculiarly well qualified to lend a hand in designing new types of family-oriented programs which could help to strengthen family life. Our tendency to oversegregate the ages, together with the numerous problems that arise from weak family life, suggest that there should be a sharper focus on services which will strengthen parents as well as children and aid the family as a whole.

Traditional programs which concentrate on serving the interests and capacities of the individual at various age levels ought to be expanded. Such opportunities for growth and development are the very essence of all that we do to carry out our commitment to help people gain their maximum potential through building inner resources and social aptitudes for functioning successfully within their families and in the community generally. All of our current operations which serve the individual go a long way toward strengthening him in this manner. But with all that we offer, underscored by the highest ideals for human betterment, we must return to the interests and needs of families to have constructive experiences as families and to mix with a community of families.

Even as we organize ourselves better to serve and advance individuality we concurrently and simultaneously should organize and promote programs designed for the family as a unit. Our present programs, with all their diversity and intense qualities of adaptability to suit individual tastes and preferences, are not quite achieving this. The common pattern is for leisure-time programs to arouse individual or age group response or participation. Though this is fine for nursery school tots, older children, and teen-agers, this line of appeal does not elicit comparable response from the parents.

Our group work and recreation agencies report that increasingly the major responsibility for managing and conducting their well-designed programs for children has fallen almost completely to professional leadership, with a staggering diminution of parental involvement in their children's social life. Parent meetings are poorly attended, and adults who join clubs and classes are less and less those who are related to the children and young people in the agency's junior divisions.

I am afraid that traditionally we have segregated the age groups partly on the assumption that they prefer it that way. Moreover, much that is good and wholesome in recreation has become so identified with children that it is shunned by adults.

Should we not be asking ourselves whether our recreational planning has become so child-centered that adults see no role for themselves, except when their children receive awards or take part in performances? A mournful lament pervades most of our agencies: "How can we get the parents?" Have we also wondered whether we are properly set up to attract them? Would programs which aim specifically at encouraging and inviting the family as such possibly be more meaningful, even more convenient, for the parents? Committed though the whole social work profession is to the basic worth and importance of the family, it is also true that much of what has resulted from our efforts to meet individual and age group needs has tended to exclude the family. Yet one of the greatest potentials for involving adults with children lies in play and recreation.

Traditional parent education courses have helped many parents. Here again, however, the content has been largely child-centered rather than parent-centered. Parents learn to be parents as demands made upon them necessitate their functioning as parents, or when opportunities arise for them to perform as parents. In addition, they have needs not only as parents but also as adults: for self-confidence, for appreciation of their instinctive wisdom, and their efforts to be good citizens. Is it at all possible for the very agencies which teach the virtues of good parental functioning also to provide good social situations where this knowledge can be used and applied in combination with relaxation and fun?

The increase in misdemeanors and delinquency among children in the seven–twelve-year age bracket is forcing us to recognize not only the breakdown of parental control but the need for parents to remain close to their children. The problem poses questions as to how our programs can more specifically contribute toward revitalizing parent-child relationships and in what areas of life our particular skills can help shore up family relationships. Henry Street Settlement's six-year demonstration project in delinquency prevention among pre-adolescent children in antisocial groups vividly and poignantly reveals how much more effective our preventive work became as the Settlement stepped up its efforts to take the parents of these children into a friendly partnership.

The most effective tools we discovered for overcoming the defensiveness and superficial apathy often encountered when parents are approached individually were the family meetings and gatherings. Here, recreation and sociability helped to draw all of us into more positive relationships.

Although we have worked intensively and separately with the children's groups, the added dimension of parental involvement has helped revitalize parent-child relationships as well as parental authority. Arousing parental interest in the children's activities through mutual participation in dances, outings, and parties has helped to build a community of parents and families around these children. This, we feel, along with the individual family work, has contributed enormously to the improved behavior of the individual children and of their groups. Parents are functioning with more confidence and energy. They are using their natural authority more consistently. The children and their friends, once the junior followers of teen-age gangs, are thoroughly enjoying the attention and concern of their parents; the parents, in turn, seem grateful for all that the agency has done to help strengthen their position in the eyes of their youngsters.

The tremendous population shift in the neighborhoods that social agencies serve has brought in families that are alone and detached, unsure of being wanted, and slow to move into the network of agencies and institutions which lead to new associations and acceptance. Isolated and often uncommunicative, they are missing one of the most fundamental experiences a family must have if it is to incorporate the community's standards—the feeling of belonging, the all-important recognition that they exist as a family and have an identity. Our separate programs for various age categories are not completely successful in drawing these families into our programs or facilities, and we cannot truthfully report that we are serving them well enough. To reach them more effectively, we may need to reorganize our resources with the special purpose of attracting the family.

The inherent and natural opportunities for family functioning in contemporary society in and of themselves are constantly changing. Though we have ample evidence that the family as a social institution is here to stay, and has something of a passion for survival, we know that functions are changing and do not altogether promote the kind of solidarity we used to take for granted. Joint and mutual activity, considered valuable in making the family a unit and useful for relieving tensions and difficulties, now requires more conscious planning and scheduling on the part of everyone.

The gradual disappearance of many of the creative tasks performed in the home has lessened the opportunity for parents and children to work together and has reduced the teaching opportunities which brought parents and children into close relationships. Whereas social training of the child for family and group participation could be expected naturally as a by-product of basic learning by doing, the lessening of teaching by parents has made the task of socialization an end in itself. External stimulation and guidance toward joint socializing experiences are sorely needed by many families.

The modern primary family in an accelerated, mobile society, minus grandmother, uncles, and cousins, has lost many of its lines of communication to the wider and busier network of social relationships in the community. The extended family in a stable neighborhood probably offered more opportunities for broader ties to other families and better chances to be recognized and known. Nothing gives a family a greater sense of pride than to hear itself described as "nice" or "lovely." The children feel a special sense of security which grows out of this kind of relatedness, especially if the family's good points are noticed. (Certainly, the grapevine works pretty well if a parent or relative gets into trouble, causing the child no end of humiliation and shame when it becomes known.) Children want their families to belong, and they treasure the chance to associate and identify with the world around them in combination with their family. There is no greater challenge to our agencies than this need to put families in touch with each other and to build bridges between them and the community in positive, productive ways.

We also have to consider what programs in some measure will offset the constantly widening social distance between the generations. Creating opportunities for whole families to plan and share new experiences together may in some small way help to cement relationships and keep the lines of communication between the generations from continually going "out of order." We find that the family-centered workshops in many of our settlements, pioneered at Henry Street twenty years ago, have met with enormous success.

Fathers and sons repair and build furniture together. Mothers and daughters make dresses for themselves. A parent and child replace soles and lifts on shoes for the whole family. These open-door programs are not graded on an age basis and have a strong tendency to induce family participation in a meaningful way. Needless to say, they meet with added success because crowded city apartments prohibit carrying on such projects in the home. We must also realize that many of our adults could not undertake these enterprises without the help of special instructors and programs which provide for learning and achievement.

Though planning and selecting programs which we can confidently say will strengthen family life is difficult and complicated, we can never overlook the rich potential within the framework of group work and recreation which are replete with ideas and goals for group participation. The very core of our daily professional tasks deals with the scheduling of services which build and strengthen character and social relationships. They constantly focus on giving groups a chance to develop good team spirit, to play and work together, to plan and create together, to participate without pressure, to gain strength through unity, to interact wholesomely with other groups. Social group work never stops trying to invent programs for so-called "secondary" groups which will produce status and carry the group a notch higher toward good morale, cohesiveness, mutuality, and dignity in the eyes of peers. We label these our most important social goals for the simplest little club organization. In other words, these are daily guide lines in planning our regular work with groups that are not families at all. We need to carry some of this idealism into special programming for families.

We must also recognize that the budgets of most of our clientele make family recreation almost prohibitive. If such experiences are valid and essential, if organized efforts are needed to promote joint family experiences, then recreation and group work agencies, public and voluntary, must make fuller provision for appropriate family services, as well as subsidizing recreational and group activities for the different age groups.

The Henry Street Settlement felt strongly enough on this subject to convert its country property, which had been operated for over fifty years as a residential camp for girls, into a family day camp last summer. Entire families—parents, grandparents, children—went off on outings together. Participation far surpassed even our expectations, and with a quality of enthusiasm that obviously represented their appreciation for a chance to get away as a family.

A whole new dimension was added to our regular summer programs. More fathers played ball with their sons than ever before; more mothers got out of the kitchen to gather their families around tables under the trees; and more neighbors learned to know each other better under pleasant circumstances and discovered common interests. None of these families, all living on the lower East Side of Manhattan, could have afforded family vacations or trips had the country day program not been available—seven days a week—at very nominal fees.

The family day camp program also made it possible to attract to the Settlement, through a single service, whole families, many of them new in our neighborhood and unfamiliar with our purposes and facilities. In a fast-changing community it is certainly more expedient and more productive to reach the whole family at once than to contact one member at a time. Is it not true that so often we have had the whole family in mind when we organized our services, only to find that we did not implement the program beyond the point of registration or intake?

I might add that the family day camp was no more costly than the resident camp, yet it served 550 families, or almost 3,000 people, rather than 240 individual girls. Though we still heartily endorse residential camping for girls and may eventually resume that program, our assessment of family needs in the light of our present community situation led us to give higher priority to a different pattern of service.

All our social agencies and institutions urgently need

to find new ways to reestablish the authority and importance of the family. To some of us it has seemed at times that we were becoming addicted to a kind of negative thinking, charging the family with being "the root of all evil," without examining closely enough the conditions which create the evil. How far, indeed, can we go in recommending recreation programs to fit the needs of the modern family if, as in some sections of this country, we are still engaged in proving that economic assistance programs are not undermining the stability of the American family? It is not enough to talk about gearing recreation to fit family and individual needs. It is the program we work for and support that will finally demonstrate the philosophy we represent—if, indeed, we have one.

Recreational and group work agencies, as community institutions, are in a sensitive position to translate the community's attitude toward family life as well as publicize any special values which the community chooses to emphasize. If we listen to our neighbors I think they will suggest to us what more we should do to achieve the social goals of our society. For it concerns strengthening and preserving the very institution which they too cherish and consider as important as life itself. Our recreation and group work services can, I feel sure, be designed and tailored to stimulate family functioning, promote family and community relationships, and contribute toward strengthening family life for a free society and its children.

COUNSELING PARENTS IN DIVORCE

by Jessie E. Peeke

THE SAN BERNARDINO COUNTY COUNCIL OF COMMUNITY SERVICES, of San Bernardino, California, a voluntary planning agency for health, welfare, and recreation programs, designed and sponsored the Divorce Project to bring to the attention of the county, state, and nation, information about "the situation of children" caught in the social and emotional complexities of divorcing parents. The Project was fortunate in having the active participation and interest of many individuals as well as that of legal, social, educational, civic, and professional organizations.

Following some preliminary studies started two years earlier, the Project has been operating since 1958 with the following purposes in mind:

1. To gather statistics about the incidence of divorce and the number and ages of the children involved
2. To evaluate techniques of assertive casework for divorcing families, aimed at helping the children in these cases
3. To examine and report findings and to recommend constructive methods of helping children and parents affected by marital stress and family disintegration resulting in separation or divorce

4. To offer assistance in augmenting and implementing the recommendations.

The Project was financed by child welfare service funds of the California State Department of Social Welfare, augmented by local funds. The Family Service Agency of San Bernardino was responsible for the preliminary studies. Interest in such an undertaking was aroused in San Bernardino County when the community became aware of the high incidence of divorce and the growing number of children affected. With a population of 503,591 in 1960, there were 18,943 divorce complaints filed in the county from 1950 through 1959. Forty-nine percent of these divorces ended in a final decree. In 1959, there were 2,129 divorce complaints filed, with 2,981 children involved. In 1960, there were 2,100 divorce complaints filed and 3,168 children affected, with an increase in the number of those under three years of age. Although there were 29 fewer divorce filings in 1960 than in 1959, there were 187 more children involved in 1960 than in 1959. The Project did not study the court records for 1961.

San Bernardino County, one of fifty-eight counties in California, covers an area of over twenty thousand square miles. It could include within its borders Massachusetts, Delaware, New Jersey, and Rhode Island and still have space. It borders to the east on Arizona, which offers easy marriage, and on Nevada, which offers both easy marriage and easy divorce, as do the border towns of Mexico less than two hours away.

The county is a fast-growing area whose population increased from 281,642 in 1950 to 503,591 in 1960, and to 514,876 in 1961. Eighty-two percent of the people live in the agricultural valley near or within forty miles of the county seat, the city of San Bernardino. Distances, and new and changing population, have presented some difficulties for effective and solid social planning.

The Divorce Project was to be accomplished in two phases. Phase I would test assertive casework through demonstration, and its findings were to be aggressively implemented during Phase II. The casework phase began in 1958 and was completed in 1960; Phase II, dealing with community organization, will be concluded in June, 1962. Seven recommendations made by the Project committee and staff have been activated, in whole or in part. When the Project terminates, there will be thirteen additional recommendations to be carried out by the board of the County Council, or other appropriate auspices.

Phase I: Assertive casework.—The demonstration for Phase I was centered in the area of the Arrowhead Social Planning Council. Names of divorcing parents were made available with the approval and cooperation of the San Bernardino County Bar Association and their member attorneys, the San Bernardino County Superior Court, and the San Bernardino County Clerk's office. Names and addresses of both parents were obtained from cooperating attorneys since this information is not part of the divorce filing. Letters offering counseling, with a brochure describing the work of the Family Service Agency, were sent to 832 parents.

One hundred and ninety-five adults were referred to the Project, 144 of whom made contact in response to the letters. Eighty-nine persons (unaccompanied by spouse) accepted counseling, while 53 separated couples each received services. During counseling, psychological evaluations and psychiatric consultations were arranged when indicated. Nineteen couples, parents of 51 children, became reconciled.

The children of the 195 divorcing parents numbered 331, of whom 181 were boys and 150 were girls. The parents represented low-middle-income families. The majority of the fathers and over half of the mothers were employed. Some 22 percent of the families were known to the San Bernardino County Welfare Department at the time of the study.

The counseling method for helping people in emotional and social distress resulting in, or due to, divorce, was tested and found valid when the Family Service Agency demonstrated that people would respond to the offer of help when they were invited, or when they were made aware that counseling services were available. Many parents said that although they had known previously of the agency services, receiving the invitation made it possible for them to apply for help. In accordance with the Project's policy, applicants were given an appointment within a week of their response to the invitation. Thus, *the service was accessible at the time of family crisis.* Long waiting lists are known to destroy interest, and often the true purpose of a community service is thereby lost.

The parents told of their personal conflicts and problems which had brought them to divorce. With some help from the counselor, they began to recognize and express concern about their children, although in the study it was found that children had low priority on the problem scale of parents. Twenty-seven of the children who were observed or interviewed had serious social and emotional problems related to the disruption in the family and to the conflicts that preceded the divorce filing. Ten percent of the project interviews were with children. Psychiatric evaluations were given to six children and psychological testing to one. Three adolescents were in serious need of psychiatric treatment. Interagency collaboration, particularly with schools, was arranged for the treatment of some children. Of primary concern to many children was the visitation of the absent parent. This points up the need for the divorcing parents to try to work out amicable arrangements for visiting, in order to promote as good a relationship as possible for the child with each parent. Divorce counseling can be of value both to the children and the parents in making such arrangements.

Of the 331 children whose parents received counseling services, there was approximately the same number of girls as boys with an average age of seven years. Most children were living with the mother. Separated fathers visited their children frequently, usually in the child's home. There were a few "Sunday fathers" who took their children to parks. Support payments were made by the majority of the separated fathers.

Nineteen couples requested counseling services in the hopes of reconciliation, and this resulted in seventeen reunited families. The project showed that reconciliation is more probable when both husband and wife are involved in counseling. In contrast to this, nineteen men and four women separately requested assistance with reuniting the family. In these cases, the mate did not accept counseling, and only two reconciliations resulted. It was interesting to note that men asked for help to reunite the family and reestablish the home more frequently than did women.

The fathers, when they had custody, were concerned with the quality of the care arranged for the children.

Mothers were concerned with the effect upon the children of the visiting father and the relationships within the family. The interviews revealed that some wives, although they really did not want a divorce, filed a divorce complaint to threaten their husbands into "good behavior." However, the filing precipitated a separation, and in some cases divorce. In contrast to this, a review of divorce filings in the San Bernardino County Clerk's office showed that some people have filed two or three times in one year without receiving the final decree. A study of these cases would be a worthwhile project.

Even when reconciliation was not reached, counseling proved important as a means of helping the clients handle some of their personal and social problems. Counseling also helped to improve parent-child relationships, diminish school problems, improve sibling relationships, and lessen contention between parents about the child's relationship to each parent.

The fact that 144 (or 17 percent) of 832 divorcing parents who received the letters of invitation requested counseling, emphasizes that people will use a service if they are personally made aware of its availability. The result of the counseling demonstrated its worth.

Phase II: Community organization.—The members of the committee for Phase I were lay and professional leaders from the Arrowhead Social Planning Council, a district council of the San Bernardino County Council of Community Services. The Divorce Project Committee was enlarged to correspond to the pattern of the San Bernardino County Council of Community Services, with all six district councils represented.

In order to extend the legal representation, the San

Bernardino County Bar Association appointed three additional attorneys from other communities in the county to the Divorce Project Committee.

The first task of the expanded committee was to evaluate the findings derived from the preceding study, having in mind two questions: In what way should our communities be improved so that family well-being can be enhanced? Is effective help readily available to families in social and emotional distress? The committee made the following recommendations:

1. An organized program of public information should be established to inform the lay public, as well as lawyers, physicians, clergymen, teachers, and social workers, of the problems pertaining to divorce and to promote greater public acceptance of the Project's recommendations.

2. The assertive technique of mailing letters to divorcing parents, inviting them to seek counseling, has proved of value and should be continued.

3. The Conciliation Court, in existence for several years, has seldom been used. This court should be strengthened and greater use of it should be promoted.

4. The advisability of establishing a Family Court which could be used in helping families and children should be studied.

5. Premarital and postmarital family life education programs should be developed. Sponsors should be found for these programs following more detailed review of existing programs.

6. Collaboration between all helping professions, especially among attorneys, physicians, teachers, ministers, and social workers, should be improved.

7. Counseling services should be improved with empha-

sis on early identification, diagnosis, and treatment of family problems.

As a result of Recommendation 1, the Public Information Committee has been of primary importance to all aspects of the Project. The committee members have worked with the local press throughout the county. They have arranged large public meetings and promoted them. They made summary brochures to tell the story of the Project in a few pages. They have secured and promoted speakers about the Project and have been effective in all facets of public information and promotion.

Stimulated by Recommendation 4 of the Divorce Project, the San Bernardino County Bar Association presented a resolution to the State Bar Association on the feasibility of having a Family Court in California. The resolution was accepted. A Family Law Study Committee was appointed and is meeting under the chairmanship of the Dean of the Law School at the University of Southern California. San Bernardino County is now in its seventeenth month of a trial experiment of having one judge of the Superior Court handle all functions that fall within a San Bernardino "Family Court."

As an outgrowth of Recommendation 5, five courses in family life education have been given in the county within the last year. Although these were not coordinated in an over-all plan, a start has been made as each community sees the need in relation to its available resources to offer courses.

Recommendations 6 and 7 have been studied by an interdisciplinary subcommittee of twelve administrators and lay people who have examined services, analyzed priorities, and isolated needs—social, economic, emotional, and legal

—which occur in families as a consequence of divorce and/ or separation. The focus of the study was: "How can services be more available and effective to one- and two-parent families to help them to be self-sustaining, or help them to maintain family dignity and strength?" This sub-committee has submitted thirteen recommendations to the County Council Board and other appropriate auspices for further study and implementation.

Although there has long been a Conciliation Court in San Bernardino County, it had been used only thirty-five times between 1939 and 1956. Cases referred for reconciliation were heard by any Superior Court judge who could work a case into his already overloaded calendar, usually late on a Friday afternoon.

Preliminary planning for strengthening the Conciliation Court included a showing of the fifty-minute documentary film *Thirty Days to Reconsider,* which is the story of the Los Angeles Conciliation Court, and a talk by the presiding judge of this court on "The Court That Pays Dividends." In addition, the Conciliation Court of Imperial County, California, was visited by the San Bernardino County Court Commission, the Director of the Divorce Project, and a probation officer of the Domestic Relations Court.

Both legal and community interest was aroused, and on January 1, 1961, the San Bernardino County Superior Court arranged with the County Probation Department to set up a pilot project, using some unexpended funds to employ a part-time conciliation counselor for eighty hours per month. The counselor and the Superior Court judge planned methods and procedures within the San Bernar-dino Court and the San Bernardino County Clerk's office for counseling couples who were considering divorce or separation. The Court drew up a conciliation agreement patterned after, and adapted from, the Los Angeles County Conciliation "Husband and Wife" Agreement.

On May 11, 1961, representatives of the Divorce Project Committee attended the budget hearing of the San Bernardino County Board of Supervisors. The position of full-time marriage counselor was approved and written into the San Bernardino County Probation Department's budget for the next fiscal year, July 1, 1961–June 30, 1962.

From January 1, 1961, to June 15, 1961, there were 92 referrals to the conciliation counselor. Thirty-four couples, or 37 percent, were reconciled, thus maintaining intact homes for 131 children. It is interesting to compare these ninety-two referrals in five and a half months of 1961 with the thirty-five referrals in the seventeen years up to 1956. From 1956 until the pilot project began on January 1, 1961, there was a similar very limited use of the Conciliation Court.

This demonstration of a service under county government resulted in the reconciliation of 37 percent of the couples. Their children will have the opportunity to be nurtured by two parents who, with help, can try again to work cooperatively for their own and their children's welfare. It is conceivable that the parents who did not reconcile gained more understanding and insight into the needs of their children through counseling.

The conciliation process stimulates many parents to think and to take another look at the problems they are creating for their children. After counseling, some parents will agree to try again for the sake of their children. However, many couples refuse to have anything to do with reconciliation, and, if pressed, they will seek other means to reinforce the need for divorce. The counselor has interviewed couples who were so incompatible that the marriage had little hope for survival. In conciliation a counselor can be very helpful in lessening the trauma to the spouses and to the children at the time of a necessary separation. Often, to do this, a referral for casework help to a community agency is indicated. This is frequently termed "divorce counseling," which is an important function of a conciliation counselor.

The joint interview with the conciliation counselor is fruitful in getting the problems stated. It has been found that one of the major issues that lead to divorce is lack of communication between spouses. Feelings run so high that it takes a third person, with a neutral and objective point of view, to release tensions and provoke discussion of the problems.

If a method were instituted for the purpose of reaching parents before legal action is started, problem-solving would be less complicated and the client more responsive to accepting help. For instance, in Imperial County Conciliation Court, instituted in 1959, if parents who are seeking a divorce have a child under fifteen years of age, they have to see the conciliation counselor before the case can come before the court. Attorneys know this and plan their cases accordingly. Imperial County feels that this policy brings about a better opportunity for reconciliation, or more effective divorce counseling.

The San Bernardino conciliation counselor sees couples referred to him, who have filed a petition for divorce or conciliation. Interviews with three couples a day constitute a full day's work. The counselor sees the couple in a joint interview to explain his function. The spouses decide which one will see the counselor first for an individual interview.

While one spouse is talking with the counselor, the other is reading the twenty-four-page document known as the "Husband and Wife Agreement." In this order the document covers: the division of responsibility; support of the family; role of the husband; the home; welfare of children; forgetting the past; a normal married life; falling out of love; work and hobbies; privacy; mutual friends; religion; love and affection; treating one's mate as the "better half"; consideration for other people's feelings; tolerance of friends and relatives; fighting; normal tone of voice; silent treatment; bearing grudges; late hours; gambling; alcohol; social activities; control of temper; nagging; mealtimes; children; normal childhood; conduct toward children; family relationships; sexual intercourse; importance of love-making; personal appearance; end-of-day problems; earnings; community funds; household expenses; family budget; pocket money; charge accounts; partnership agreement; and family prayer.

Following the first individual interview, the counselor talks with the other spouse, while the one already interviewed reads the "Husband and Wife Agreement." This is followed immediately by a second joint interview focused on the possibility of compromise based on the document just read. If they come to an agreement and sign the document, the final procedure is a discussion by the couple and the counselor with the judge of the Conciliation Court. With the judge's signature, the document becomes a court order. After the period of a year, there will be a follow-up of the effectiveness of conciliation counseling.

The County Clerk's office has had an active role throughout the Divorce Project activities, including working with the staff in assembling statistics, in representation on the Divorce Project Committee, and in handling the calendar for the conciliation counselor. Encouraged by the successes of the conciliation counselor and the effectiveness of the "Husband and Wife Agreement," they devised in June, 1961, a twenty-page brochure called *Not Only "I Do" but Also "I Agree,"* to be given to couples who apply for licenses to marry. This brochure, another form of assertive technique, contains educational material concerned with the responsibilities of marriage, advises counseling where needed, and lists books and pamphlets for homemakers which are available in the San Bernardino city and county libraries.

The Project proved that some parents who filed for divorce responded favorably to assertive techniques and were willing to accept casework help. The report of the conciliation counselor showed that using the "Husband and Wife Agreement" was effective in bringing about better understanding and insight between spouses. Both proved that even after a petition for divorce is filed, it is *not too late* to try casework methods. In both settings, in a voluntary family agency and in an official court, parents did respond to counseling, gained insight and understanding about their children and themselves, whether they reached a reconciliation or not.

The Project illustrates the importance of interprofessional and citizen collaboration about the problems provoked in the divorce process. Committees studied problems, made decisions, and carried out recommendations. Professional groups, the Bar Association, and the courts have encouraging evidence of accomplishments.

Whether, as a result of the Project, the incidence of divorce will decrease we cannot say. We can say that community education and interprofessional and lay collaboration have laid the groundwork for continued service and stimulated community interest in such.

SERVICES TO THE FAMILIES OF HANDICAPPED CHILDREN

by Helen M. Wallace, M.D.

THE UNITED STATES NATIONAL HEALTH SURVEY conducted in 1957–58 estimated that there were 9,000,000 children under fifteen years of age who had a disabling physical condition. Of this number, approximately 700,000 were limited in their activities as a result. About 600,000 children had a partial limitation of activity, and about 100,000 children had a major limitation of mobility; that is, they had trouble getting around outside the home without help. Another 58,000 had a critical mobility limitation; that is, they were confined to the house all of the time except in an emergency. About one third of the impairments found in children under fifteen years of age were orthopedic, one quarter were speech, one seventh were hearing, and one twelfth were visual.

Reactions to the presence of a handicap in a child vary considerably. Some children and their families seem to be able to accept the handicap and manage well with it, or in spite of it; other children and their families are not able to do as well. While there may be some relationship between the degree of the child's handicap and the ability to cope with it, this is not invariably so. The key to the situation appears to be the basic parent-child relationship —whether the child feels loved, wanted, and is reared with consistency in discipline so that he feels secure. While this is of course true for all children, it becomes even more important for the child who is handicapped.

Some children who are handicapped may feel that they are different from, or inferior to, normal children. This may be especially true if the child has been kept isolated at home and has not had the opportunity for socializing experiences with other children. The feeling of isolation is especially typical of the child who is homebound because of a severe physical disability or who is blind or deaf. For example, a profound hearing loss in a very young child frequently interferes with his ability to communicate with others, and hence he may miss some of the usual give-and-take which is a normal part of growing up in a family. A handicapped child may feel resentful and that he is the victim of an injustice.

Separation of the child, particularly an infant or pre-school child, from his family may be psychologically traumatic. The handicapped child may react by reversion to infantile habits, such as bed-wetting, or by withdrawal and failure to respond to people. Such physical separation occurs when the young child is hospitalized or placed in a residential institution. Preventive steps consist of avoidance of unnecessary hospitalization or institutionalization of young children; and when hospitalization is essential, there should be adequate preparation of the child and his family for the step. Liberal and flexible visiting hours for the parents are necessary.

Another type of reaction occurs when the child is rejected by his family because of his handicap. When such maternal deprivation exists, the handicapped child may also react by regression to infantile behavior, by withdrawal, or by being hostile and aggressive.

Still another reaction is that of increased dependency. This may occur particularly when the child has been overprotected by his family and not adequately encouraged to learn to care for himself and to become independent. Learning to do things for himself, an essential part of the normal development of the nonhandicapped child, is equally important for the child who is handicapped.

Dependency is fostered when the child has been unable to attend school. The lack of an adequate education is significant for the child of any age—both for the educational and the socializing values derived. It becomes particularly frustrating for the handicapped adolescent who sees other teen-agers able to accept employment but who is himself excluded from such opportunities. This adds to his feeling of dependency, of being different, of being inferior to others.

While many families love and want their handicapped children and do their utmost to accept them and to help them to develop to their maximum potential, this is not true of all families. The basic need is for acceptance, love, encouragement, assistance, and consistency in rearing.

Some parents who have a child with a congenital handicap become anxious and concerned about future pregnancies. The basic need here is to help the parents express their feelings and to accept the facts. This not only requires knowledge, but also time and tact in presentation. Long-term counseling is usually necessary.

At times, the reaction of parents to having a handicapped child is a feeling of guilt. Parents may look upon this as punishment or retribution for something, imaginary or real, which they may have done in the past. Or they may feel resentful and antagonistic because this has happened to them and unconsciously act out their resentment in the care of their child. In another type, conscious or otherwise, one side of the family may blame the other side for what has happened. In any event, marital harmony may be disrupted and further difficulties ensue.

Still another family reaction may be rejection of the child. The parents may, for example, isolate the child in a room and be unwilling to take him out of doors. Part of this reaction may be associated with a feeling of shame that they have a child who is handicapped. In the past, this feeling was particularly prominent when the child was epileptic, mentally retarded, or cerebral palsied. As more knowledge and understanding have developed and education of the public has increased, this type of reaction has become much less prevalent. On the other hand, rejection of a handicapped child may assume more subtle forms and may consist of neglect of the child within the home or infrequent visiting when he is hospitalized or institutionalized; at times it may even be the cause of failure to pursue treatment and therapy. Another manifestation is rejection of the child's diagnosis and the subsequent "shopping around" from one physician to another.

At the other extreme, parental reaction may consist of overprotection of the handicapped child, even to the point of neglecting normal siblings. This is seen when parents pour out everything they have—time, effort, energy, funds, and interest—on their handicapped child, and therefore have little left over for their other children.

Associated with many of these situations is the fact that

the handicapping condition of many children, particularly those who are moderately to severely disabled, may last for many years and frequently for the duration of the individual's life. Long-term care is essential, and such care is often necessary on an intensive, day-to-day basis. This may place a tremendous physical burden on the family, especially on the mother. The task of lifting a heavy, disabled child may become too great a physical strain. Added to this is the social and emotional drain on the family when the child needs constant care and attention and the mother may rarely, if ever, be able to escape from these demands for recreation of her own.

Related to the need for long-term care is the fact that such attention is usually expensive. This, then, adds a financial burden to the physical, psychological, and social drain.

Information concerning the physical and emotional growth and development of normal children is requisite for any professional who works with handicapped children. Such information is necessary for early case-finding, accurate diagnosis, prescribing for short-term and long-term treatment and rehabilitation, timing the details of these plans, and carrying out steps designed to foster secondary prevention of potential additional handicaps. Certain principles serve as an inherent background to this discussion:

1. Children are constantly growing, developing, and changing. This means that continuing health care of infants and children is of great importance in supervision of these changes, in assistance and advice to parents regarding child rearing, and in early observation of deviant development and behavior. The fact of continuous growth and change

is one of the major reasons for frequent periodic reappraisal of the status of each handicapped child and his family, to ascertain the changes which may necessitate any modification in his rehabilitation program.

2. There is a general pattern of growth and development of children. For example, normal infants and children learn to sit up before they learn to stand, and to stand before they walk. Another example is that hearing is essential for normal speech and language development.

3. Each child grows and develops in his own unique way. While his growth pattern, in general, may resemble that of other children, the time table is strictly his own.

4. The tempo of growth is not even.

5. There are periods when a child is ready to achieve his next step. This principle can be useful in working with the child and in guiding his parents. Until a child is ready, training in any particular activity may be useless and may even establish negative feelings toward the activity which may retard later training.

Infancy.—From a broad point of view, how the mother and father of a newborn infant with an obvious abnormality react to him depends on the thinking, planning, and emotions with which they went through the pregnancy. Even more broadly, their reactions are a reflection of all the experiences which have been incorporated into their lives prior to the pregnancy. The disparity between the ideal infant hoped for and the actual reality of their baby can set up a number of possible reactions in the parents, ranging from grief to dissociation and inability to give physical care and to form a close, loving, warm relationship with their infant; to denial of the condition; and to unrealistic overprotection. From a practical point of view, the most urgent needs, when an infant is born with an obvious abnormality, are those in which the social worker plays a major role—assistance to parents in learning, understanding, and accepting their child's diagnosis and its implications; opportunity to discuss this as thoroughly as the parents are ready for it and as repeatedly as is needed by the parents; emotional support; and assistance in planning and in working through the plan.

The basic concept of growth and development is that the quality of parental care which a child receives in his earliest years is of vital importance to his future emotional health. It is believed to be essential that as infant and young child he experiences a warm, intimate, and continuous relationship with his mother (or his permanent mother substitute), in which both the infant and his mother find satisfaction and enjoyment. If the infant is deprived of this quality of relationship on a continuing basis, that is, if the infant suffers from maternal deprivation,[1] the potentiality exists for the development of emotional ill-health. Deprivation may be complete, in that the infant is removed from the continuous care of his mother or mother substitute, as in a hospital or institution, or it may be partial and take on the more subtle form of maternal rejection. It is thought that the period of greatest vulnerability to maternal deprivation exists in infancy and early childhood, although the vulnerability between three and five years of age is still serious. After the age of five years, vulnerability diminishes, although a fair proportion of children between the ages of

[1] J. Bowlby, *Maternal Care and Mental Health,* World Health Organization Monograph Series No. 2 (Geneva, Switzerland: 1952).

five and eight years are unable to adjust satisfactorily to separation, especially if it is sudden and if there has been no preparation.

The practical implications of these concepts relate to the plan of treatment and rehabilitation of handicapped infants and children. For example, wherever possible, they would live and grow up at home with their family. Unnecessary hospitalization would be avoided. When hospitalization is indicated, there would be preparation of both the parents and the child, and the period of hospital stay would be as brief as is medically and socially permissible. During hospitalization, parents would be able to visit as often as necessary. Care of a personal rather than an impersonal nature would be provided by the hospital staff. In East Africa, when a child is hospitalized, one of the parents usually moves into the hospital with him, a trend slowly occurring in the United States.

During infancy and childhood one of the basic needs is that of satisfying hunger. Thus, the type of feeding and the feeding situation assume major importance. One of the basic drives is the need for pleasure in sucking. The infant with a harelip and cleft palate may have great difficulty in feeding. Not only is there the hazard of aspirating the food, with a possibly fatal outcome, but also there may be lack of sucking gratification. The practical application of this information is to instruct the mother in the techniques of feeding these infants so that both nutritionally and emotionally their growth and development will be fostered.

By the middle of the first year of life, the normal infant is already reaching out for and grasping objects, and learning to transfer objects from one hand to the other. This series of milestones has implications for the treatment of infants with congenital amputation of the upper extremity. Formerly, it was held desirable to fit the prosthesis when the child was about four and one half years of age. However, in the Grand Rapids congenital amputee center, it was decided to fit the child as soon as he was examined. Infants as young as five months of age have been successfully provided with a prosthesis.[2]

By their first birthday, most normal children are well on their way to standing and beginning to take a few steps. This knowledge of normal children is used, whenever possible, in treatment of children with disability involving the lower extremity. For example, children of this age with paralysis of the lower extremity due to cerebral palsy or *spina bifida* are encouraged to assume an upright position, and, if necessary, they are fitted with braces. The principle involved is, of course, the application of the usual timing of a specific step accomplished by normal children to the rehabilitation of handicapped children.

The preschool period.—This is the time when the normal child is slowly developing independence. Play occupies an important part of the preschool child's life. It is important for parents to permit their child enough independence, combined with guidance, to make possible the most constructive use of his inherent capacities. During the middle and latter part of the preschool period, socialization experiences may be helpful for many children. For the handicapped preschool child who may be somewhat restricted

[2] C. H. Frantz and G. T. Actken, "The Habilitation of the Childhood Amputee," in *Proceedings of the Institute on Prevention and Management of Handicapping Conditions in Infancy and Childhood* (Ann Arbor, Mich.: University of Michigan School of Public Health, 1959), pp. 142–66.

in his activities, opportunity for socialization may be an important aspect of his rehabilitation. Opportunity to participate in a day care or nursery school program is being more and more frequently provided for handicapped preschool children for this reason. Also, admission of some handicapped preschool children to special day classes in school is encouraged in many communities for the same reason.

During the preschool period, the normal child is acquiring mastery of certain basic skills, such as toilet training. When the handicapped preschool child is ready, bowel and bladder training represent an important aspect of his developmental program, in preparation for school admission.

Illness and hospitalization are particularly disturbing experiences for the preschool child and regression may occur. As evidence of anxiety there may be loss of bowel and bladder control or increased need for thumb or finger sucking. There may also be fear of surgery and mutilation. The comments previously made in regard to hospitalization during infancy apply also to the preschool child. The provision on the hospital ward of adequate play outlets and group experience and the opportunity for the child to verbalize his fears or misconceptions regarding treatment are constructive techniques.

During the preschool period the mother plays an important teaching, guiding, and supervisory role. This usual maternal role presents an opportunity, therefore, to include the teaching of the mother in the training and rehabilitation program of her child. For example, many of the simpler techniques of physical, occupational, and speech therapy can be taught to the mother so that she, in turn, can carry them out in the home on a continuing basis.

The preschool period is normally one of rapid speech and language development. This, of course, is the reason for the timing of speech therapy for children with cerebral palsy, cleft palate, or a moderate-to-severe hearing loss, to capitalize on the characteristic time of normal speech development.

The use of knowledge of physical growth in the rehabilitation of the handicapped preschool child can be illustrated by the child with cleft palate. We have previously cited the need for speech therapy beginning with the early preschool period. Retention and protection of the preschool child's teeth becomes an important aspect of the treatment program for a variety of reasons: for development of intelligible speech; for chewing; for facial appearance; and for preservation of the normal space relationships for eruption of the permanent teeth. In addition, some children will require the deciduous teeth to aid in the retention of prosthetic appliances. Thus, early and continuing dental care is essential for the preschool child with cleft palate. Furthermore, increasing knowledge about growth of the mouth and jaws has led to delay for surgery to close the cleft in the palate, in order to permit more growth of the palatal structures prior to surgery.

The school-aged child.—From the time of usual school admission until adolescence there is steady emotional and physical growth and development, proceeding at a more even pace than in infancy and the preschool years. The early part of this period has an important milestone for most children—entrance to school. While there is significant individual variation in the degree of emotional maturity of these children, nevertheless most are able to operate with some independence toward their family.

Growing independence is characteristic of this period, permitting the child to explore outside his own family circle, especially in his own peer group. Group activities begin to play an important role in his life—Cub Scouts, Brownies, church or neighborhood group, baseball, hobbies. This is the time when numerous and complex motor skills develop. The child presents a picture of almost ceaseless activity. The teacher plays an important role and can have enormous influence; the sense of identification is prominent, and the school child may identify with the teacher or, perhaps, in the case of boys, with one of our astronauts. There is great need for a feeling of accomplishment and great pride in accomplishment.

A tendency to regression may occur in the school-aged child. This may be associated with illness, hospitalization, surgery, or the birth of a sibling.

The presence of a handicap in a child of this age may assume major importance. Some children become over-anxious and overdependent; others attempt to deny the existence of any illness or disability. While obesity is more common during adolescence, it may also occur in handicapped children of this age group and is related to inactivity, overeating, and insufficient interests, possibly associated with a feeling of frustration.

One of the most important needs for the school-aged handicapped child is to be able to live at home and to attend school as other children do. Wherever possible, it is desirable that the child attend classes in as normal a school setting as possible. In other words, the handicapped child needs to be integrated into the regular school system, with the program adopted or modified to meet his needs. This includes placement in a regular class or, if this is not feasible, in a special day class. Careful evaluation of the child and of his abilities and potentialities is indicated at the time of school admission, including equal attention to the psychosocial aspects. Frequent periodic reappraisal is equally important, in order to meet the individual child's changing condition and needs. Where there is a sufficient number of handicapped children to warrant provision of a special day class or day school, usually a team of specialists is needed, including a social worker.

Another aspect to be kept in mind is the need to provide for the recreational needs of the school-aged handicapped child, again in as normal a setting as possible. Opportunity to participate in the community's and school's recreational programs for normal children is desirable in so far as it is possible.

Adolescence.—Adolescence is the period of rapid physical growth, physiological changes, and emotional growth.

For many youths, adolescence is a time of storm and stress. The adolescent demands increased independence, but at the same time he demonstrates dependency needs as well. One of the main characteristics is the search to clarify who he is and what his role in society is to be. Major questions in middle-class culture are: "Will I be able to go to college? Will I be able to get in?" Those who are unable to go to college must consider vocational training and future employment.

The adolescent is typically conscious of, and greatly occupied with, his physical appearance. Adolescents are especially aware of height, weight, acne. Girls are concerned with the growth of the breasts; boys, of the genital organs.

Adolescents tend to form cliques, groups, clubs, or gangs. Great emphasis is placed upon relationships with their peers, and upon similarities of dress and gestures. The adolescent is typically a "joiner" and engages in many activities, such as dancing, athletics, school paper, debating, and so on.

One of the major interests and areas of concern to adolescents is that of relationships with the opposite sex and the handling of the intensified sex drives. It is said that an earlier and more determined experimentation with sexual relationships takes place now than formerly. This has resulted in "going steady" at a younger age in order to avoid promiscuity. One of the phenomena of the past two decades has been the increase in early marriages, as well as in out-of-wedlock pregnancies.

All these characteristics of the normal adolescent may be aggravated in the teen-ager who is handicapped. Essentially, the major concerns are with education, training, future employment opportunities, physical appearance, social relationships, and recreational acitivities. As one mother of a not too badly handicapped cerebral palsied youth said recently, "When Leonard was young, we had little problems; now that he is growing up, we have bigger problems." When I asked her what she meant, she described the problem of selecting a college which was reasonably good and which would take him. Having hurdled this obstacle successfully, the more immediate one has been the difficulty of his finding girls to take out. The ultimate problems will be those of employment and marriage. Although the boy is physically handicapped, he is one of the more fortunate ones since he is able to get around quite well with a cane.

There is an urgent need to expand present resources and make available early vocational testing, guidance, training, and placement for handicapped youth. At the same time, a sheltered workshop program is necessary for those who will require protected employment.

Recreational and social outlets are another facet of rehabilitation for handicapped youth. Here too, wherever possible, integration of the handicapped into the usual activities of the entire peer group is desirable. It is helpful to build into this some provision for assisting the handicapped teen-ager with his grooming.

It is clear that change is the basic characteristic of growth and development of children, and that the changes are both physical and emotional. Awareness of such changes in each handicapped child is essential if rehabilitation techniques are to be properly timed. Intimate knowledge of each child and his family are necessary so that the concept of readiness may be applied to his rehabilitation program. It is important that the child be able to handle each phase of his development as successfully as possible, to pave the way for the next phase. From a practical point of view, this means a comprehensive evaluation of the child initially, and repeated reevaluations so that the program may be adapted to his needs at a particular time. Comprehensive care includes not only the maximum improvement of the child's physical condition, but equal attention to the social, emotional, educational, vocational, and recreational aspects. It is unusual to be able to provide this quality of care, except in a team setting.

EARLY DETECTION OF EMOTIONAL DISTURBANCE IN A WELL-BABY CLINIC

by Pierre Johannet, M.D.

FOR SOME YEARS I have participated in the well-baby clinic of the James Jackson Putnam Children's Center. This clinic was established in 1949 by one of the Center's co-founders, Dr. Marian Putnam. Its original purpose was to provide the Center's staff with an opportunity to study normal mothers and infants by means of direct observations in order to shed light on the earliest phases of the mother-child relationship and also to attempt early prevention of emotional disorders. Since that time systematic research projects have evolved, and a second well-baby clinic was established for the pursuit of more formal research goals. The original clinic has continued to function, although on a smaller scale. Its main emphasis is on training child psychiatrists and on the less formal research. It is with this latter aspect of the well-baby clinic activities that I have been connected.

The problem of early detection of emotional disturbances in infancy is an important issue much in keeping with the current emphasis on the preventive aspects of mental health. The need for more knowledge in this area is clear. Not long ago, Anna Freud, restating some aspects of an important article written by Ernst Kris in 1950, re-minded us that the diagnosis of emotional disturbances in childhood "usually comes too late when the disturbance has become massive . . . and that the dividing line be-tween normality and pathology is too easy to miss." [1] She reemphasized the difficulties encountered in trying to predict pathology for the purpose of early intervention and the need for further intensive research in this area.

For many years pediatricians, public health nurses, and other child care workers have had to grapple with this problem. Workers in child placement agencies have been actively engaged with decisions regarding the emotional health of the very young child. They often are reduced to making an educated guess. They are well aware how dif-ficult such decisions can be. It is true that the majority of mothers and children we have observed at our well-baby clinic functioned well within the range of normal mental health; even then we may have noted occasional transient and self-limited deviations and had to decide whether to fit these into the normal spectrum. But we have also en-countered situations in which deviations in development became progressively worse—sometimes rapidly, sometimes slowly and insidiously—until active intervention helped to reverse the trend. Such experiences are not, I am sure, restricted to our own clinic.

The position of the community well-baby clinic in deal-ing with this problem is unique. Early detection of mal-function is one of its traditional roles within the larger scope of preventive medicine. Much has been accomplished

[1] Anna Freud, "Child Observation and Prediction of Development: a Memorial Lecture in Honor of Ernst Kris," in *The Psychoanalytic Study of the Child* (New York: International Universities Press, 1958), XIII, 92.

in the area of physical health. The prevention of mental illness, however, is still in an early phase. The relatively common occurrence of emotional disturbances even in young children is now being recognized. The more serious of these form one of the common groups of severe childhood diseases. If we consider their potentially malignant impact on the child's total development, the seriousness of these disturbances is indeed a matter to be reckoned with. The psychoses and psychosomatic illnesses probably have their origin in the first year of life even though the illness may not reach its full development until much later; there is increasing evidence in support of the concept that these illnesses are related to an early severe disturbance in the mother-child relationship. But we should not consider only the most severe disturbances. A chronic sleep disturbance in a baby under one year of age will not, alone, produce a psychosis, but it can do much to undermine the possibility of the comfortable and satisfying relationship between mother and child so essential for the development of a healthy personality.

We are concerned with all types of emotional disturbances which can occur during childhood. We want to know how early a team of professional observers, sensitive to the nuances of developmental patterns, can spot the signs of trouble. In the course of diagnostic studies of a very young child suffering from neurotic disorders the family pediatrician is usually asked for his opinion of the child. Occasionally, the report will indicate that while the pediatrician has been aware of a disturbance, he felt that it was chiefly in the mother and that she was the one in need of psychiatric treatment. It is perhaps true but only half true. Psychiatric disorders do not take the same form in very young children that they do in adults or older children, and for that reason they are often missed. These disorders usually first appear as slight deviations in normal functioning, or, for example a lag in maturation, fussiness around eating, disturbances in the sleeping pattern, anxious crying in response to noises, or hyperactive behavior. Deviations might be seen in children otherwise normal; if such is the case, these deviations may well be transient and leave no pathological aftereffects; their disappearance may occur spontaneously, or the mother may do something to help the child over a difficult state, independently or with the supportive guidance of a pediatrician or child care worker. Why is it that such apparently benign deviations go on, in some cases, to assume the distressing proportions of a fully developed emotional disorder? We think that the answer is to be found in an evaluation of the total environment in which they begin to appear.

Studies based on direct observations of mother and child have gone a long way toward confirming hypotheses based on psychoanalytic reconstructions in the treatment of adult and child patients. One of these hypotheses states simply that the mother and her baby form a dynamic unit. It is not simply that the mother molds her baby into certain patterns nor that, as some have argued in the case of the autistic child, an innate disturbance in the child has altered the mother's previously normal personality. Rather, as we have learned to understand it, the mother and her baby enjoy a mutually influential interaction to which both partners bring their own specific contributions; there occurs a kind of mutual regulation leading to adaptation or maladaptation, depending on the case. Constitutional factors in the child play an important role. The result will not be the same if the infant's disposition meets with certain expectations in the mother and if it runs counter to such expectations. Of course, a mother's ability to adapt to a variety of situations, the degree of flexibility which she brings to this relationship, is also important. The mother's attitude will, of course, be determined in large part by her basic personality structure and by certain specific unconscious attitudes and fantasies related to her child; these may have their roots in unresolved conflicts with her own parents and may find expression in the new relationship to her child. Current emotional stresses and their impact on the mother must also be considered; depression sometimes occurs following childbirth or may develop in the wake of an important personal loss. The role which the father plays is also crucial in the way he relates both to his wife and to his child.

The factors I have so far enumerated combine to form what Mrs. Beata Rank has termed the "emotional climate" of the child. There is no single standard of favorable emotional climate. It should, however, provide a mutually satisfying relationship in which the mother develops a sensitive understanding of her baby's evolving needs and an ability to recognize correctly her baby's growing capacity to tolerate certain frustrations. This is maternal devotion in the true sense of the term and will lead to development in the child of a basic sense of trust.

The emotional climate is specific for each particular child and may vary a good deal from child to child within one family. This is because the factors which enter into it are not the same. No two children are the same nor do they have the same meaning to their mother in terms of her conscious and unconscious attitudes toward them. Although it is not usually easy to determine this at first glance, interviews with the mother will eventually give us a greater understanding of these special meanings of a child to the mother. Such an understanding will prove very useful in those cases where we detect trouble and are trying to help the mother to modify her behavior sufficiently to permit a successful adaptation.

An additional factor that bears on the emotional climate has to do with a common cultural pattern of this age. Young parents tend to be very mobile and often move away from their families and familiar environment. This may leave them emotionally unprepared for the crises of pregnancy, childbirth, and parenthood. It can create a certain degree of tension in the early emotional climate of the infant; but in the less pathological situations tension will eventually give way to increasing security. This perplexity in the parents needs to be differentiated from the deeper anxieties which are the result of ambivalence and of intense unresolved conflicts in the mother. A woman's need for emotional support during the early stages of motherhood is natural. Feelings of inadequacy may become magnified if the young parents are isolated from those toward whom they could look for support and for approval.

We now turn more specifically to the actual evidence of disturbance in the child—the deviations in development and the symptomatic behavior. These are the signs which indicate the existence of an imbalance and make us scrutinize more closely the emotional climate from which they arise.

The ways in which an infant responds to emotional trauma are limited; the range of reactions comprises regressions and fixations in the development, retardation in the acquisition of skills or loss of certain recently acquired skills; disturbances of vegetative functions, such as eating and sleeping; changes in the level of activity, with either hyperactive behavior or marked passivity; anxious and excessive crying. These rather limited responses are in contrast with the quickly growing resourcefulness that a normal infant in a favorable emotional climate will show in handling the minor tribulations and frustrations of daily living.

The assessment of developmental deviations is not an easy matter. Although there are known maturational time-tables, there are also many normal variations. For instance, some babies will walk earlier or talk earlier than expected; the opposite also happens. Either one may be a result of the child's constitutional endowment. Mental retardation, which is easily recognized later in childhood, presents during infancy a difficult diagnostic problem; it may not be until the child is well into his second year, in some cases, that one can be certain about it. When we see extreme discrepancies, we soon become suspicious that we may be dealing with a disturbance in the emotional development of the child. There is, of course, little doubt when we encounter the fully established patterns of profound disturbances such as occur in the atypical development found in the so-called "early childhood" psychoses, but we would want to be able to spot the earliest signs of such disturbances before the characteristic pattern of isolation and withdrawal becomes too firmly ingrained. Recognizing these signs is not easy. Attempts to reconstruct them from the history of cases where the disease is well-established present a difficult problem. We usually have to rely on observations made mainly by the parents during the child's early development; and these, of course, are subject to the vicissitudes of memory, that is, forgetting, repression, distortion. The emotional development of an infant is, in part at least, a function of the integration of many individual elements—maturation of perceptual functions, motor skills, coordination, and so on. Occasionally, discrepancies occur in this integration. For example, we sometimes see babies who can sit up and creep and yet are unable to bear weight, although there is no doubt that they have sufficient strength to do so. We assume that the weight-bearing posture gives rise in these children to certain tensions probably related to conflicts, which, to be understood, must be seen in a total context.

Certain signs, such as the smiling response to the sight of the human face which appears sometime between the ages of two and five weeks, are well-established guideposts to the normal development of young infants. Their failure to appear we see as an index of disturbance, again to be assessed in the context of the child's emotional climate.

Disturbances in the vital functions of eating and sleeping are common in infancy. In the milder forms, much can be done to help correct such situations. Some mothers who complain that their children will not eat may be trying to force excessive amounts of food on them, or they may be trying to accomplish other tasks while feeding their children. In either case, this tends to turn mealtimes from pleasurable experiences into periods of harassment for both mother and child. The child gradually becomes disinclined to eat. If these facts were known it would be relatively simple for the child care worker to provide the mother with an adequate solution. However, mothers rarely volunteer such additional information, and it is up to the alert worker to obtain it.

We have heard mothers complain that their babies will not go to sleep and cry in their cribs for long periods of time if they are not picked up. In some cases we may learn the following: The child's father sees the baby briefly in the morning for a quick rough-and-tumble session which is repeated just before bedtime. At night, then, the child, in a state of excitation, expects more, wishes to maintain this excited state, and cries in angry frustration when put down in his crib. To this mother we would stress the importance of quiet before sleep. Reading to the child at this time, even though he may not understand, provides a lulling, rhythmic background that prepares him for sleep by reducing his expectation of stimulation and encouraging him to turn, in part, toward himself for comfort, thus establishing a state conducive to sleep.

I realize that I have only partially presented the range of disturbances in infancy, but I believe it offers a broad idea of what we think constitutes a disturbance. In order to differentiate between the more and the less pathological we need to evaluate, not only the tenacity, as it were, of the disturbances, but also the range of functions affected and especially the quality of the emotional climate in which they arise.

Although the setting of our well-baby clinic is quite different from the usual setting of a community clinic, it might suggest ways in which these clinics could adapt themselves for the purpose of detecting early emotional disturbances.

The mothers are referred to us from the community by the visiting nurse association or other sources. The clinic meets once weekly, and the mothers are encouraged to come every week during the first few months after delivery; later, they are asked to come every other week. They are aware in a general way of our scientific interest and of our need to have them attend regularly. The staff consists of pediatricians, psychoanalysts, psychiatrists, psychologists, and trainees in child psychiatry. In addition to getting the usual services of a well-baby clinic, the mothers are interviewed by the physician who is in charge of the case. The rest of the time, which runs to an hour and a half, the mother spends in our well-baby room talking informally with other mothers and with members of our staff. The psychologist records his observations of the child's behavior and responses in this informal setting. Following this, the staff meet for an hour to discuss their observations of the mothers and children.

I am aware of our emphasis on having a staff capable of noticing psychological nuances. We do not feel that it is necessary to have a staff of trained therapists. But it is indispensable that the observers be aware of psychological aspects of development if they are to detect the early signs of emotional disturbances. It would seem that psychiatric social workers would be a very useful complement to such a staff.

The case which I have selected from our well-baby clinic files illustrates problems which appeared early and continued to progress without spontaneous remission. The intervention by the pediatrician demonstrates a situation in which the lighter approach was sufficient to bring about a reversal in a pathological trend.

Sam N. had been brought to our well-baby clinic when he was nearly seven weeks old. His rate of weight gain in his first year of life was so rapid that his birth weight could have approximately sextupled during that time, in contrast to the usual rate of tripling or quadrupling the birth weight. In addition, although he gave the impression of being an active baby in the early weeks, he became more and more lethargic so that we were increasingly concerned about his development. We thought of this in terms of two hypotheses: (1) that the mother for a number of reasons wished for a quiet, unobtrusive baby and endeavored with alarming success to encourage his passivity; and (2) that this very quietness reduced his caloric usage so that he gained weight overly rapidly on a relatively normal caloric intake. Mrs. N. herself found it difficult to tolerate any discussion of either the inactivity or the obesity of the infant despite comments from strangers about her son's weight when she took him with her in his carriage while shopping. We became convinced that the careful, slow, and tactful intervention of the pediatrician would be paramount in preventing a potentially serious problem.

The mother had come to the clinic to take part in a research project dealing with the development of children's play and their attachment to transitional objects. She cooperated actively, especially in the physical care of her son and in aiding our direct observations. However, we came to understand that she was much more than ordinarily reticent in regard to emotional matters. We would be able to offer only largely unsupported conjectures as to the causes of her particular personality development; but we were able, through our leisurely, frequently repeated observations of her ways of caring for her child during his physical examinations, and her discussions with the pediatrician, to see certain patterns of thinking and feeling about her child, of interaction with him, and to hear from her how she dealt with the normal problems of feeding and the expected increase in her son's motility as he grew older.

At birth Sam had weighed 6 pounds, $7\frac{1}{4}$ ounces and his length was $19\frac{1}{2}$ inches. On initial physical examination the boy was described as normal. The mother told us of having felt confident before delivery of her ability to care for him, but spoke of herself as having lost confidence afterward. She was unhappy in staying at her mother's home for the first two weeks following delivery and found it a relief to return to her own

apartment with her husband. Sam was bottle-fed. Our first examination took place when he was six weeks old, at which time
Sam already weighed 10 pounds, 14 oz. When the baby was eight
weeks old, and weighed 12 pounds and 8 ounces, we learned that
the mother usually gave the bottle to Sam while she was watch-
ing television, and so far as we could learn this was the usual
pattern henceforth. We understood this as indicating the
mother's need to receive in order to be able to give to the
child as well as representing her need to control his activities.

When Sam was ten weeks old we began to note the rapidity
of his weight gain; he weighed 14 pounds, more than double the
birth weight. We also observed an occasion when the child
was unhappy and was given milk by his mother. We wondered if
this were part of a pattern whereby the mother used milk and
feeding as a solace.

At twelve weeks he weighed 15 pounds, 4 ounces. We made a
prediction that the mother would become angry if her son refused food. Approximately a year later we began to hear con-
firmatory evidence, such as the mother's statement that she
had to fight with him about eating cereal.

As time went on, we became more and more concerned about
the child's rapid weight gain and very limited motor activity.
However, as the mother clearly needed to control the subjects
that were talked about, these topics could not be discussed. Mrs.
N. had numerous questions to ask the pediatrician at each visit,
particularly about inoculations and other aspects of physical care.
To the psychiatrist she gave principally descriptions of the baby's
play and accounts of difficulties in getting the boy to sleep at
night.

The skin care she gave to her child was of the finest. His
clothing was meticulously clean. Her attention to what he was
allowed to put in his mouth was most notable. She related that
she washed his toys each evening, and her reluctance to allow
her son to use the playthings provided in the clinic was unusual.
The latter seems to have reflected her doubts about the clinic's
permissiveness, and her need to stay away from matters concerning emotions.

At approximately six months of age Sam weighed 24 pounds,

6 ounces. At eight months he weighed 29 pounds. The pediatrician was able to raise some questions about quantity of food intake in relation to Sam's extremely rapid weight gain. In the following months the idea of using skim milk instead of whole milk was presented by the pediatrician, a woman in whom Mrs. N. appeared to place the most trust, and in repeated discussions she was aided in implementing this suggestion. We do not think she reached an intellectual awareness of the effects of her own particular method of bringing up her child, but she was able to make enough modifications so that Sam's weight by the end of the second year was within the normal range—30 pounds, 4 ounces—and his activity had increased by leaps and bounds.

This case illustrates how an emotional imbalance in the mother-child relationship can be reflected in the physical development of an infant, and how the alerted members of a well-baby clinic might deal with such a problem.

Physical signs of emotional imbalance may reflect deeper psychological problems. Space does not allow us to present such cases. However, it will suffice to add that the more time-consuming approach of classical psychotherapy is indicated only when measures such as this one illustrated in the case reported above fail to bring about change. The alert worker trained in the appreciation of psychological problems of development is in a position to detect such deviations early in an infant's life and take the appropriate steps.

DISCUSSION

by Charlotte Tejessy

AS A CASEWORKER, one sometimes wonders what sort of infants one's clients might have been, which is quite unanswerable. Or, at least, answers would be limited since reconstructive material by necessity is incomplete, full of holes and distortions. Therefore, there is satisfaction in the idea of starting from the beginning—or almost the beginning—of human development and posing the question: What kind of child and adult will we get given a certain baby, a certain mother, a certain father, and a certain constellation of environmental influences? It has been intriguing to review some of the literature in preparation for this discussion, to think about the applicability of our increasing knowledge of early childhood development to social casework, and to react to Dr. Johannet's material.

In my private child guidance work with parents during the past year, I became more and more aware that I was drawing heavily on my participation in my friends' experiences with their infants and children. What I had observed, almost unwittingly, during those neighborly leisure-time visits worked its way to the forefront of my mind during my interviews with mothers whose difficulties with their children I tried to understand and help. Why? Why did not my knowledge of the personalities of the mothers, the way they presented their material, what I knew about the psychiatrist's work with the child, and all the things I had read about child development, suffice? Why did I seem to go back again and again to situations where I was right in the middle of the lively involvement of a mother and her child? Was there something missing in my interviews with the mothers which was present during those personal experiences on Saturday afternoons in the backyards of my friends? In a certain sense I knew my friends better than my clients. I had absorbed along the way information from many different sources—what their pediatrician had said about the infant's constitution; the mother's own medical problems; the mother's expectation in regard to her child; current emotional stresses of the family; the mother's adapt-

ability in meeting the child's demands; the family's social
and vocational aspirations and cultural background; the
mother's conflicts with her own mother. And from the
mother's behavior over the years I also had received
glimpses of her unconscious attitudes and fantasies regarding her child. Furthermore, by just being there, I had tuned
in on the nonverbal communications between mother and
child to an extent impossible to achieve in an interview
with the mother alone.

I hope that what I have described, using partly his own
words, restates correctly Dr. Johannet's central thesis,
namely, that one needs to assess the emotional climate of
a child before one is able to consider questions of normal
growth, of deviation from such growth or the tricky problem of prediction.

Caseworkers, particularly those who work in a family or
adoption agency, have all made home visits, have observed
mothers and their small infants, and are in a sense con-
tinuously engaged in the assessment of a specific child's
emotional climate. This is part and parcel of our practice.
But unless we are directly involved in a research project,
dealing with an investigation of the mother-child relationship and early personality development, we are rarely asked
to study the emotional climate of a child systematically. I
have used the illustration of my friends and their children
in order to highlight from everyday experiences—since
most of us do not work in well-baby clinics as yet—those
facets of a complex situation (the mother-child relationship) which make up the basic ingredients of our most
rigorous research in early childhood development.

At this point I should like to mention the longitudinal
study of early personality development, begun at the Boston

University School of Medicine—Massachusetts Memorial Hospitals Medical Center in 1954, as an example of the type of intense ongoing research in this area which may serve as a conceptual and practical framework in our attempts to delineate the emotional climate of a child and trace the beginnings of pathology. In following this quotation from the most recent article to come out of this study, please keep in mind the question: How is knowledge derived from research in early childhood development useful to us as caseworkers?

The study was of a naturalistic exploratory type, planned to provide frequent opportunities to observe mother and child together in a variety of situations over the first six years of life. Most of these observational situations were structured quite consistently from contact to contact. Only primiparous mothers were selected to keep the factor of mothering experience comparable in the groups. Detailed descriptions were made at each contact of the behavior of the mother, of the child, of the interaction between them. Thus, for each mother-child pair a longitudinal descriptive account was obtained of the progression of outstanding characteristics their interaction demonstrated in these well defined situations over the years of the study. Comparable observations have been gathered on twenty-two of the mother-child pairs from birth through the thirty-sixth month of life.[1]

The group has begun to analyze this extensive interactional material, and one of the avenues of approach to this task which they are following at present

consists of dividing the interactional data gathered for each pair into a sequence of time segments and making evaluations of interactions prominent in each segment. . . . these evaluations [are used] to study the proposal that in this early period there

[1] Louis V. Sander, "Issues in Early Mother-Child Interaction," *Journal of the American Academy of Child Psychiatry*, I (1962), 141.

are a series of issues that are being negotiated in the interaction between mother and child.[2]

(I shall omit here the theoretical considerations and the observational material which have suggested such a possibility.)

[The group's] observational material of the first eighteen months of life seemed to fall into five large time segments, each with a prominent feature which was encountered extensively in the data for that period. The first period corresponds to the "undifferentiated phase" of early ego development (Hartmann, Kris, & Loewenstein, 1946), namely, the first two and a half months of life. . . . A central issue in these months concerns the degree of specific appropriateness the mother can maintain in her response to the cues the baby gives of his state and needs. The second period, from two and a half to five months, is the segment most thoroughly described by Spitz and Wolf (1946), in which smiling behavior is developing and coming to play a central role in the relationship. The degree to which truly reciprocal interchanges are established between infant and mother has been selected for evaluation. The third period between five and nine months has interested us especially in regard to the way in which the baby's expression of initiative for social exchange and for various preferences is responded to by the mother. . . . The fourth period, between nine and twelve or thirteen months, has been delimited somewhat more arbitrarily.[3]

The feature of interaction most impressive to the investigators during this phase "concerned the intensity and insistence with which the child made demands on the mother and the manner in which she dealt with them." [4] The demands of the child during this phase become focalized on the mother.

The fifth period, extending from the twelfth to the eighteenth month, has been described in detail by Erikson (1950) in relation

[2] *Ibid.*, p. 141–42.   [3] *Ibid.*, p. 144–45.   [4] *Ibid.*, p. 145.

to the establishing of early autonomy. We have been especially interested in evaluating for each mother-child pair precisely how the self-assertion of the child is dealt with, particularly when it is in opposition to the mother's wishes.

By arranging the data according to these time segments, descriptive features of the observations can be compared in different subjects at roughly the same point in the life of the child. Individual variations in the chronology of significant interactions then become apparent.[5]

Research in early childhood development is going ahead full steam and our clinical application of this increasing knowledge must follow. It is a question of time only. For caseworkers the implications, I believe, are twofold: those relating to diagnosis and therapeutic intervention, and those relating to training or social work education.

Dr. Pavenstedt, the chief investigator of the above-mentioned study, feels that we do not have "sufficient data to be able to state with any degree of security what it is we should support and what forces are disruptive enough to warrant our making a decisive effort to combat them." [6] What we have learned increasingly is to identify signposts of everyday child behavior. Thus, when a mother tells us about her infant, her relationship to her baby, we should know as caseworkers what questions to ask and we should consider what she tells us in the light of what we have come to understand as "normal" interactions; not from the point of view of the baby alone, or the mother alone, but as a dynamic process. Furthermore, we need to reconstruct the feelings in these interactions in order really to understand, and with this I think I am in agreement with Dr. Johannet.

[5] *Ibid.*

[6] Eleanor Pavenstedt, "Study of Immature Mothers and Their Children," in Gerald Caplan, ed., *Prevention of Mental Disorders in Children: Initial Explorations* (New York: Basic Books, 1961), p. 192.

What did not become so clear to me from his paper has to do with the very question of deviation from normal development. It seems to me that we do know a lot about normal variations, that is, from a cross-sectional point of view. We know when a baby should sit up, and what percentage in a random sample of the population sits up later or earlier. We may know the causes of such variation quite well; what we have a harder time knowing are the consequences. We do not know what will happen later on to a baby who does not sit up at the normal time. It is the longitudinal variation about which our knowledge is still meager. The question of what are the longitudinal consequences of variations in normal infant development and mother-child interaction remains difficult to answer.

Dr. Sander has stressed that even though the group working on this research did not attempt to influence the natural course of development of these mothers and their children, the factor of continuity of contact with them seemed of great importance. The mothers in the study received real concern for them personally from the group though nobody tried to advise them. Dr. Pavenstedt thinks that

if a similar sustained interest could be maintained for mothers from their first appearance in the pre-natal clinic, through delivery, and into the child's early years at least, a strong bond would be established that would be invaluable to young mothers who have little or poor contact with women experienced in the mothering role.[7]

For example, if prenatal and well-baby clinics were adjacent, with closely knit personnel, mothers then might

[7] *Ibid.*, p. 205.

remain in touch with the same professional group. Most physicians in well-baby clinics—the James Jackson Putnam Children's Center being an exception—will have too little time to give this kind of attention to "normal" mothers. One might envision that caseworkers with specialized training in maternal and child care would be permanently attached to prenatal clincs, well-baby clinics, and pediatric wards, making an effort to establish and continue contact with those mothers whose pressing needs and troubles in relation to the care of their children have to be met in order to prevent more serious difficulties later on.

Dr. Johannet's clinical material could, of course, be discussed from many different angles. Thinking of the professional caseworker, it occurred to me that our customary way of offering help to clients will need, perhaps, to be revised. We are used to having troubled people go to any number of social agencies and ask for help. The responsibility of asking for help rests primarily with the client. There is little question in my mind that Sam's mother needed professional help. Mrs. N., while cooperating in the physical care of her son, was reticent in regard to emotional matters and there seems to be hardly any indication that she was aware of having an emotional problem in relation to this child. Yet, help she needed—she did not know how to ask for it other than to continue bringing the child to the pediatrician. I do not believe that she could have accepted a referral to a professional person outside the well-baby clinic. Therefore, a caseworker would need to be attached to the well-baby clinic—that is to say, if a caseworker rather than the pediatrician were to attempt to help this mother work out some of her problems.

I would like to raise the question as to whether research in early childhood development might lead us to intervene even earlier than was done in the case of Sam.

Let me present briefly a few thoughts in relation to my second point: the implication of our knowledge of early childhood development for social work education. In our teaching of early childhood development at the schools of social work we need to inculcate a greater feeling of what transpires between a mother and her child. Direct observation and participation by the student in nursery school and community well-baby clinics may be one avenue of approach. Another might be that whenever home visits are made by casework students more attention could be given to observational data in relation to a mother's interaction with her small infant. Furthermore, while schools of social work teach students to be on the lookout for the cultural backgrounds of their clients' families, perhaps more concentrated attention could be given to specific cultural variations in child-rearing practices. Social workers, in general, know a lot about family life, and this knowledge could be most helpful should we extend our services to community well-baby clinics.

One further point occurs to me. I think I am correct in stating that in many schools of social work, pediatricians and child psychiatrists teach information from their respective fields; but this material often is taught quite separately. Thus, the burden of integration is left primarily to the student. Could we give more thought as teachers to the problems of integrating such material by combining the different facets of early childhood development into a more meaningful whole? I feel compelled to finish this discussion with a word of caution, however. Our increasing knowledge of early childhood development must not tempt us to use prematurely what we learn in our work with clients. This is particularly true for social work students, who in their enthusiasm may misapply such new knowledge. Much of what we have learned and will continue to learn needs to be used indirectly by the caseworker by helping her understand better the mother she is treating and by giving her clues to each mother's special kind of need.

THE FAMILY AS THE UNIT OF SERVICE IN SOCIAL WORK

by Dorothy Bird Daly

IN RECENT YEARS, the social work profession has been taking a new look at one of its oldest concerns and seeing it in a new light. The family has become the nexus of the field of social welfare. Its task has been defined as the identification and elimination of social forces inimical to good family life; the development of individual capacity to function effectively in appropriate family roles; and the fostering of a culture that will support the family in the fulfillment of its function as the primary social institution. In the broad sense, these are the tasks of our whole society, and of all its social institutions. In a technical sense, however, they are the specific concern of social welfare institutions and agencies. Social welfare is dedicated to the strengthening of family life for individual and social goals.

What are the implications of this clarification of purpose for the professional practice of social work? How can we translate these goals into services? If the field of social welfare as a societal institution has thus defined its purpose, what has been or should be the effect of such definition on professional method?

Social work practice has been engaged in a struggle at least since 1915, and probably for years before that, to identify its unique place among the professions. Abraham Flexner in his historic presentation at the National Conference of Charities and Correction in that year conceded that:

> The activities . . . are obviously intellectual, not mechanical, not routine in character. The worker must possess fine powers of analysis and discrimination, breadth and flexibility of sympathy, sound judgment, skill in utilizing whatever resources are available, facility in devising new combinations. These operations are assuredly of intellectual quality.
>
> I confess I am not clear, however, as to whether this responsibility is not rather that of a mediating than an original agency.[1]
>
> . . . We observed that professions need to be limited and definite in scope, in order that practitioners may themselves act; but the high degree of specialized competency required for action and conditioned on limitation of area cannot possibly go with the width of scope characteristic of social work. A certain superficiality of attainment, a certain lack of practical ability, necessarily characterize such breadths of endeavor.[2]
>
> Lack of specificity in aim affects seriously the problem of training social workers. Professions that are able to define their objects precisely can work out educational procedures capable of accomplishing a desired result. But the occupations of social workers are so numerous and diverse that no compact, purposefully organized educational discipline is feasible.[3]

In 1929, the Milford Conference made an heroic attempt to grapple with the problem of definition—but was not successful in distinguishing the essential nature of social work from other forms of professional work:

[1] Abraham Flexner, "Is Social Work a Profession?" in *Proceedings of the National Conference of Charities and Correction*, 1915 (Chicago, 1915), pp. 584–85.
[2] *Ibid.*, p. 586.   [3] *Ibid.*, p. 587.

At the present time the practice of social case work is more precise than the formulations of philosophy, knowledge, methods and experience. . .

The remedy for the situation in the judgment of the Committee is clear. Social case workers must become more energetic in pursuing penetrating study and research in their professional subject matter. We believe that this report outlines a content for social case work sufficiently substantiated in its implications to justify the claim that social case work is potentially both scientific in character and professional in its practice. Scientific and professional, however, are terms which can at the present time justifiably be applied to social case work chiefly because of its potentialities.[4]

In 1961, Harriett M. Bartlett showed that the profession was still struggling in this confusion.[5]

In 1944, M. Robert Gomberg wrote:

. . . when family case work accepts as its focus a responsibility to the whole family, it defines a useful uniformity of purpose, structure, and method in spite of the large variety of problems and services with which it deals.[6]

I would suggest that we delete from Dr. Gomberg's paragraph the words "family case work" and substitute "social work."

When social work accepts as its focus a responsibility to the family it defines a useful uniformity of purpose, structure, and method. In other words, it arrives at a delineation of its particular and unique contribution as a societal institution and professional function.

[4] *Social Case Work, Generic and Specific* (New York: American Association of Social Workers, 1929), p. 11.

[5] Harriett M. Bartlett, *Analyzing Social Work Practice by Fields* (New York: National Association of Social Workers, 1961).

[6] M. Robert Gomberg, "The Specific Nature of Family Case Work," in Jessie Taft, ed., *A Functional Approach to Family Case Work* (Philadelphia: University of Pennsylvania Press, 1944), p. 147.

It may be helpful to review the path I traversed in arriving at this theory. It originated in my occupational concern as Director of Field Work at the New York University Graduate School of Social Work, in the development of a specific curriculum for the field work sequence. Field work is a most important, indeed an indispensable, segment in the education of a social worker. Social work demands of the practitioner a substantial body of scientific knowledge and theory which has been identified and can be taught to the student through classroom instruction, observation, research, and reading. But to be of service to another human being, the social worker must incorporate this knowledge and learn to use himself as the major tool of his method. Hence, social work takes on the attributes of an art, and competency in the practice of an art can be accomplished only by practice itself.

The knowledge of the nature of human personality and behavior, of social structure and society, of individual and societal pathology, and the skills of case and group analysis and professional communication and intervention through the helping process and the professional relationship must be so incorporated into the person of a social worker that his use of them in his interaction with his clients becomes intuitive and spontaneous. The student's increasing knowledge from class and library comes alive and becomes the means of helping others only as the student experiences the phenomenon he has heard described in class or learned about through reports of research.

Because of the nature of social work itself, this practice sequence must be carried out in a real agency with real clients, rather than in a laboratory or by means of role play. As Bertha Reynolds said so well:

We start . . . from a belief that life is infinitely varied, dynamic, and changing, and that social work is . . . an integral part of life. It can be understood only as it is seen in relation to all other living forces of its time, and only as its growth is traced through a past, in which it had significance, to the promise of its future.[7]

It is out of this conviction that our school is committed to a program of concurrent field work and class instruction, and to a field work experience for each student that is integrally a part of the living, changing social agencies of our time. We are not looking for the rarefied atmosphere of educationally controlled student units in laboratory settings where the student is protected from the noise and dust and confusion of life in an agency. The more completely the student is integrated into the day-by-day operation of the agency, the more responsibly he functions as a representative of the agency, the more complete will be his development as a social worker. This is not to say that he becomes an apprentice worker, carrying a share of the service commitment of the agency. His reason for being there is to learn, and hence his educational experience must not only be protected but must be carefully planned to provide the learning that is essential for his development. Meeting both these needs simultaneously is no easy task.

We had been giving considerable attention to this aspect of the field work program this past year, both in faculty committees and in our meetings with the field work instructors. We had earlier spelled out the broad educational goals and the more immediate purposes of the sequence. Our concern, now, was to establish the specific curriculum of the practice sequence itself.

[7] Bertha Capen Reynolds, *Learning and Teaching in the Practice of Social Work* (New York: Farrar & Rinehart, Inc., 1942), p. 3.

Gordon Hamilton, who, in her new role of elder states-man, is continuing to put the spotlight of her keen intelligence on the weaknesses in our profession, devoted an editorial to this question. She says:

. . . let us not forget that the basis of professional qualification *always* remains in practice. The range and methods in field instruction are still far too uneven and far too often narrow and insubstantial. . . . the characteristic which distinguishes a profession from the sciences which underpin, inform, yet can never contain it, is the integration of theory with the highest level of practice . . .[8]

Katherine Kendall, in 1959, at the fiftieth anniversary dinner honoring social agencies that have participated in the field work program of the School of Social Service Administration of the University of Chicago, raised as one of the principal issues facing the field, the need to assure reasonable uniformity in the learning opportunities offered in field practice:

Is field teaching an individual matter between supervisor and student, subject to all the variations of capacity and interest which inevitably exist when many people are used as field instructors? Or does field teaching have more characteristics in common with classroom teaching than we have yet recognized? Could we, perhaps, develop more precise guides to teaching in the field in order to insure adequate coverage of essential concepts and principles and a minimum standard of proficiency in the use of problem-solving procedures?[9]

Harriett M. Bartlett poses the same problem:

Field work teaching of social work students is an educational activity but providing field work opportunities and experience

[8] "Editor's Page," *Social Work*, VII, No. 2 (1962), 2.
[9] Katherine A. Kendall, "Selected Issues in Field Instruction in Education for Social Work," *Social Service Review*, XXXIII (1959), 6.

is a responsibility of social work practice and thus closely tied in with the development of that practice. It is generally agreed that field instruction as used in social work represents an educational invention of significance and value. Its place in the whole curriculum and the results that can confidently be expected from its use have not, however, been yet determined with enough precision.[10]

An important task facing education for social work is the identification of learning experiences that will be likely to attain the educational purposes we are seeking to accomplish. At this point, it seems necessary to recall the introductory statement of the basic premise on which our field work curriculum is organized. Here we said we believed in student practice in the living, changing social agencies of our time, not in laboratory settings, even if such existed. But when we seek the advantages for student learning inherent in such settings, we face, head on, a dilemma to which there is no easy solution. One of the major characteristics of our profession historically has been the fact that social work developed in distinct ways in several fields of practice. Not until 1929, at the Milford Conference, was there any clear delineation of the generic and specific nature of practice. Not until 1955 did the membership come together in a single professional organization. In 1952, education for social work, after several years of development, established a generic curriculum; and in 1958, approval of specializations for fields of practice was discontinued. Curriculum and course content became truly generic, with the exception of a separation for the three primary methods courses—casework, group work, and community organization.

[10] Bartlett, *op. cit.*, p. 62.

Field work, however, has not kept pace. The student experience tends to reflect too much the specialized approach to problem-solving characteristic of the particular field with which his agency is identified. We now need to define the field work experience in sufficient specificity that we can be sure that all students are having certain essential learning experiences. I finally arrived at a way of accomplishing this with which we are experimenting in our school.

All students will have a core case load of families in order to work with, and observe, parent-child, marital, and sibling relationships; to see the family in its milieu and to gain a true understanding of the psychodynamics of family life and the role of the family in social structure. Students will then have experience with differences in age and sex roles, with a variety of ethnic and subcultural groups, and with the effect of living conditions and economic hardships on family life.

We have chosen family-oriented practice as the cornerstone on which to build our field work curriculum for several reasons:

First, it provides the means of effectively integrating class and field.

In the "Human Growth and Behavior" sequence, the student is taught that the family is the basic social institution. The most important components of personality, those on which all progress in life depends, come into being in early childhood in the give-and-take of family life. The struggle between trust and mistrust is worked out in relationships between the parents and infant; autonomy and initiative are developed in action and counteraction of the young child in the family.

The sense of identification, so important a development of adolescence, emerges in relation to status in the family. The capacity to love and be loved, to form attachments and develop relationships; the capacity to accept authority in its rightful place—all these emerge in large measure from the kind of relations that obtain within the family. In its economic function, a sense of material values, for good or bad, is developed; opportunities and advantages or their reverse depend in large measure on the regularity, amount, and source of income of the family.

Not only normal development, but physical and psychic pathology are family-rooted:

The main determinants of neuroses are social—that is, essentially familial in origin. Character disorders do not exist alone; they function in pairs and threesomes. For every person suffering from a character disorder, there are one or more partners who share the pathology. They are a social, as well as an individual, phenomenon. Mutual and complementary acting out is frequent in contemporary family patterns.

The neuroses of the various family members reinforce one another through family contagion. Treatment for individual's problems is complicated because resistance is continually fortified by the emotional situation in the family. Sometimes, the client is virtually the prisoner of an unhealthy familial role. To accomplish change, the family must change along with the client.[11]

Dr. Ackerman urges us toward the integration of our concepts in personality theory and toward the design of a broader frame of reference within which it is possible more effectively to conceptualize and treat an individual's disturbances within the matrix of his position in his primary group—the family.

[11] Nathan W. Ackerman, M.D., *The Psychodynamics of Family Life* (New York: Basic Books, Inc., 1958), p. 33.

In the "Social Process" sequence, the student is taught the basic sociological and anthropological concepts of value in social work practice in relation to the community and the group. This includes the nature of culture, and the place in it, of norms and values, beliefs and moral standards, methods of problem-solving and communication. American values of independence and individualism are considered in relation to their impact on the unemployed, ill, handicapped, and disabled client. Society, social structure, and social role are studied as ever-changing networks of relationships among people. Emphasis is placed on study of the family as the basic unit of society, and social role within the family and the family's role in, and dependence on, society are developed. Subcultures and their impact in the family are considered; cultural pluralism in the American scene and the effects of family mobility and culture conflicts are emphasized. The importance of seeing difference without signifying it an aberration in relation to the establishment of treatment goals for families or groups is considered.

When we recognize that it is through the family that the child gets his first sense of what is allowed and what is forbidden, what is valued and what is despised in the society or section of it of which he is a part; when we see that the way in which the culture's requirements are transmitted to the child determines what use he will make of them and how successful he will be in his relation to them, we face very clearly the need for experience with families to integrate this knowledge. It is through the family that the client enters society and becomes identified with his community. The dependence of the family on the supporting culture to reinforce its defenses and shore up its weaknesses and the effects of breakdown in this area must be fully learned by the student of social work, and can be learned only through field work.

In relation to the sequence of courses in social policy and programs, the student is taught that the unifying purpose of national social policy is to strengthen the family, a primary social goal of a free society. The student is taught that the social welfare task is the identification and elimination of social forces inimical to good family life and the development of services to support the family in the fulfillment of its function in a free society. It is within this context that our students learn about the social security system, the social insurances, government-sponsored housing measures, public health and mental hygiene services.

To summarize, then, our first reason for family-oriented field work is that substantive course content is so oriented, and we have here the key to integration of the curriculum.

The methods courses are, of course, closely interwoven with the field work sequence. Every student in the methods courses is required to be concurrently in a field work placement. The methods teachers who serve as faculty advisers to students in field work are closely related to the agency in which the student is placed; consult regularly throughout the year with the field work instructor—both in relation to the content of the experience and the progress of the student—and sustain also a relationship with the student, helping him in the integration of his classwork with his field experience. In addition, the several areas of practice are represented in each of the methods sections, and illustrative material from the field is used for discussion in these classes, which are kept small in order that there can be full participation of all the students at each session.

In addition, the methods sequence serves to reinforce

the student's integration of content from his other courses in the development of his own theoretical base of practice. The methods course focuses on the social work process, structured within the framework of basic concepts, such as the use of social role concepts which draw heavily on familial roles and the social role of the family, social functioning, and family interaction. The classes study, too, how to understand clients and family through a knowledge of social functioning.

The importance of interviewing clients in their homes and the necessity for understanding the impact of the community on the family are emphasized. Needs of families are studied in relation to the identification of social problems, community attitudes toward categories of problems, and the role of society in the perception of a problem in relation to its effect on the people concerned. The concept of communication and the distortions in diagnoses that can occur because of faulty communication emphasizes the need for family interviews and observation. The concept of prevention is related to understanding the total family. The student is taught not only how to treat the pathology of the individual client but also to study the family to identify sources of immediate or incipient problems in other members so that preventive service can be given on an extended base. The primary client may or may not represent the most serious pathology in the family, and, unless the student knows the total family, he may fail to identify family strengths. Effort is made to broaden the vista of the student to see the problem in larger focus, to understand why these families have these problems, and to see the relation of individual family problems to community needs.

For all these reasons, family-oriented field work for all

students would strengthen immeasurably the effectiveness of the methods sequences.

The second reason grows out of our learning theory and our experience in seeing how the student changes from a layman to a social worker. Becoming aware of oneself—one's feelings, attitudes, and prejudices—is perhaps the most serious adjustment in thinking that a student faces in field work. Awareness of self means facing, perhaps for the first time, awareness of one's feeling toward one's own family and objectively analyzing one's own family role.

Since the origin of these feelings, attitudes, fears, and prejudices are in the family relationships of the student, he can come to grips with them in the struggle toward professionalization; he can see them in microcosm if he has an opportunity in the field to be responsibly related to family interaction and family problems in relationship.

This is a particularly necessary experience for the young, recent college graduate who is just breaking away from childhood dependency as he moves into graduate study. But it is also valuable for the older student who is involved in family relationships as spouse or parent.

A third reason for this formulation is that services to families in both casework and group service agencies run like binding threads through the whole pattern of social work, historically and in the current scene. Family orientation is possible in all fields of practice and in all methods.

We are proposing, then, for these reasons, that all students will have a core case load of families in both the first and the second year, in both casework and group work, and in all fields of practice. In these cases they will see the family as the unit of work, even though the service of the agency is directed toward only one member, such as a member of a settlement house group, an offender on parole, or a child or aged person in placement.

In these cases, the field workers will have responsibility to know and be in communication with several family members. They will make home visits and have opportunity and responsibility to observe marital, parent-child, and sibling relationships. They will be responsible for studying the subculture of the neighborhood and community and its impact on the family and the impact also of the family's economic functioning and living conditions.

Treatment may properly still be focused on the individual, either because it is the method of choice or because agency functional limitations prohibit family treatment, but such individual or group treatment should develop out of family study and diagnosis.

When this proposal was presented to the executives of the Council of Teaching Agencies affiliated with New York University, and debated and deliberated upon in round-table discussion, there was a wide variety of responses. Consensus was that the focus on the family could serve as an integrating and cohesive force in the identification of a generic base for social work education. Question was raised as to the advisability of such a student experience if it were not in conformity with agency practice generally. This question was then extended to discussion of why the theoretical base presented for this proposal was not equally applicable to professional social work practice per se. A discussant from a general hospital (with medical, psychiatric, and rehabilitative services) and one from a community center settlement house demonstrated its desirability and its logic, from their own experiences, in a family-oriented program in medical social work and in a traditional group work setting.

If services to strengthen family life in both casework and group work agencies run like a binding thread, if knowledge of the importance of the family in the health of the individual and society, known empirically to generations of social workers, is now substantiated by science and research, then may we not seek to institutionalize this knowledge and function as the particular, universal identification of professional practice?

PAPERS PRESENTED AT THE 89TH ANNUAL FORUM MAY ALSO BE FOUND IN *The Social Welfare Forum, 1962* AND IN *Social Work Practice, 1962,* BOTH PUBLISHED BY COLUMBIA UNIVERSITY PRESS.

DATE DUE